DISCARD

*The Fifty Finest Athletes
of the 20th Century*

To the librarians and research specialists
of this world—especially Una Shih

The Fifty Finest Athletes of the 20th Century

A Worldwide Reference

by

ROBERT J. CONDON

McFarland & Company, Inc., Publishers
Jefferson, North Carolina, and London

British Library Cataloguing-in-Publication data are available

Library of Congress Cataloguing-in-Publication Data

Condon, Robert J., 1934–
    The fifty finest athletes of the 20 century : a worldwide
reference / Robert J. Condon.
        p.   cm.
    Includes index.
    Summary: Profiles superachievers in thirteen different sports,
grouped in the categories "The Top Twenty," "The Runners-up," and
"The Greatest Athlete of the Twentieth Century." ∞
    ISBN 0-89950-374-8 (lib. bdg. : 55# alk. paper)
    1. Athletes – Biography.   2. Athletes – Rating of.
[1. Athletes.]   I. Title.
GV697.A1C67   1990
796'.092'2 – dc20
[B]
[920]   89-43643
                                                            CIP
                                                            AC

Manufactured in the United States of America

McFarland & Company, Inc., Publishers
  Box 611, Jefferson, North Carolina 28640

Table of Contents

v

Table of Contents

The Greatest

Introduction

This book tells the stories of many fine athletes. It is divided into two sections, the top 20 athletes of the 20th century, and the 30 runners-up.

To qualify in the top 20, or even the top 50, in a century, the athlete has done one or more of the following:

1. Achieved a level of performance that has yet to be equaled.
2. Played a sport so well that subsequently it was played differently.
3. Dominated a sport for a decade or more.
4. Was indisputedly the best to have competed in a given sport.
5. Played several sports extremely well.

The selections are one person's opinions and he agrees that many great performers were omitted from the list. Imagine a list of top athletes that does not include Grover Cleveland Alexander, Cy Young (he actually had 265 of his 508 wins in the 19th century), Lefty Grove, Jack Johnson, Rocky Marciano, Henry Armstrong, Bronco Nagurski, Jean-Claude Killy, Dick Butkus, Hank Aaron, Lawrence Taylor, Bjorn Borg, George Mikan, Carl Lewis, and so many other superstars? It's a tough cut.

Although the list includes competitors from 13 sports, baseball has a higher number of selections than other sports, probably because the game has been the national pastime for most of the century and the better athletes naturally gravitated to it. Baseball's main competitor for paying customers for the first fifty years of the century was boxing. Football was almost strictly a college sport until the emergence of television coverage in the late 1950s, and golf and tennis were considered "rich men's sports." Most fans today would not recognize basketball as it was played in the 1930s and 1940s, before the jump shot, pro 24-second clock, and fast break.

American athletes also dominate the selections. Throughout the century, people in the United States made a living from sports, while professionalism in other parts of the world is a relatively recent development. Moreover, two world wars retarded athletic development in most of the world more dramatically than it did in the United States.

One premise in the selections is that a great athlete of the 1920s would be a great athlete today and vice versa. Walter Johnson could still pitch today and Ruth would hit.

The decade of the 1990s will produce more challengers. Among the current competitors, two are certain to be "top 50 athletes" by the year 2000; three others are probabilities and an additional two are on their way.

Certain

Joe Montana. Joe's leadership, passing and Super Bowl rings while performing for the San Francisco 49ers in the late 1980s and early 1990s should earn him the accolade "Finest Quarterback of All-Time."

Magic Johnson. Johnson's extraordinary seasons with the Los Angeles Lakers at the end of the 1980s have established him as one of the finest basketball players ever.

Probable

Michael Jordan. Jordan does things on a basketball court that have never been seen before. He needs to lead the Chicago Bulls to an NBA championship to solidify his position as a "top 50" performer.

Lawrence Taylor. The New York Giants' L.T. will be considered the finest defensive football player in the history of the game when he retires. Opposing offensive coordinators design their game plans to try to minimize the effect of Taylor's charge and pursuit from the outside linebacker position.

Bo Jackson. Bo already has a Heisman Trophy and is a star in both baseball and football — an astounding fear in this era of specialization and overlapping seasons.

On the Way

Mike Tyson. Iron Mike's express train to boxing immortality was temporarily derailed by Buster Douglas in 1989. Mike must rebound as Joe Louis did after Max Schmeling caught him unprepared or go the route of two other previously "invincible" heavyweight champions, Sonny Liston and George Foreman.

Steffi Graf. Graf compiled the finest record for a teenager in the history of tennis. She has the game to be the best woman player ever but meet the challenge of a strong group of younger players led by Monica Seles and Jennifer Capriati.

The number of great athletes still competing and yet to compete by the year 2000 creates the problem as to which great athletes to delete from the list. Perhaps the solution is to expand the honor roll!

So let us celebrate the performances of these great athletes who have added so much to the enjoyment of so many people.

The Top 20

Kareem Abdul-Jabbar

Born: Ferdinand Lewis Alcindor, Jr.
April 16, 1947–

When Lew Alcindor was a youngster growing up near the northern tip of Manhattan Island, neighborhood kids used to push him around because he was skinny and not aggressive enough to take care of himself. When he started playing grade school basketball, his classmates laughed at the gawky kid who spent much of his court time falling over himself. But by the time he was in high school they stopped laughing, and today not too many old acquaintances are prepared to give Kareem an elbow in the ribs to test his reaction. For over 24 years, Lew Alcindor, now Kareem Abdul-Jabbar, has been a dominant factor in college and professional basketball.

Kareem first gained attention when he starred in basketball for Power Memorial Academy, a Catholic high school on the west side of Manhattan. With Kareem leading the way, Power Memorial had 71 straight victories in New York City's powerful Catholic High School League and won the national high school championship for two consecutive years. The team's only loss during Kareem's tenure was to perennial basketball powerhouse DeMatha High School from Hyattsville, Maryland.

Kareem chose UCLA for college largely out of respect for its peerless coach, John Wooden. From 1967 through 1969, his three years of college eligibility, UCLA won the NCAA championship three times and Kareem was chosen the NCAA's Player of the Year in each of those years. While at UCLA, he converted to Islam and changed his name to Kareem Abdul-Jabbar.

Kareem was drafted by the Milwaukee Bucks of the National Basketball Association in 1969. He immediately quieted those critics who thought he could not handle the bulky NBA centers by winning the league's Rookie of the Year Award for the 1969–70 season. The lowly Bucks had won only 27 games the year before Kareem joined them, but improved to 56 wins in Kareem's rookie season. Milwaukee obtained the aging but still effective all-time professional, Oscar Robertson, in the following season, and Robertson and Jabbar became one of the most powerful combinations in professional basketball history.

3

Jabbar's skyhook — a virtually impossible shot to block. (Courtesy of the Milwaukee Bucks.)

The 1970–71 Bucks were among the greatest basketball teams ever assembled. With Oscar playmaking and Kareem scoring an average of 31.7 points per game, the team compiled a 66–16 regular season record, and at one point reeled off 20 wins in a row. The Bucks swept the Baltimore Bullets to win the NBA playoffs, and Jabbar won the first of his six league Most Valuable Player awards. The Robertson-Jabbar combo was broken up before the 1973–74 season when Oscar retired and Kareem was traded to the Los Angeles Lakers, along with Walt Wesley, for four players.

Within a few years, the Lakers became the class of the National Basketball Association along with the perennial front-running Boston Celtics. Jabbar regularly averaged 25 points per game and the Lakers won the NBA championship in 1980, 1982, 1985, 1987 and 1988, and were

Opposite: **Kareem Abdul-Jabbar was a dominant college basketball player at UCLA. His teams won 3 consecutive NCAA titles. (Courtesy of UCLA.)**

runners-up in 1983, 1984, and 1989. Kareem again had the good fortune to be teamed with another great backcourtman, Earvin "Magic" Johnson. Perhaps Kareem's finest moment in basketball occurred with the 1985 Lakers when the balding, 38-year-old veteran sky-hooked the vaunted Boston Celtics into submission, and was recognized as the playoff's Most Valuable Player, an honor he previously won with the Bucks in 1971.

Some athletes seem to be winners, but few were better at it than Kareem. During his career, Jabbar's teams won 70.7 percent of the games in which he played. This includes four years at Power Memorial where his teams were 95–6, four years with UCLA whose teams were 109–2, and for his first 19 years spent in the NBA, Kareem's teams were 1,205–576. Kareem played on only two teams with losing records, his last season with the Bucks and his first with the Lakers.

At the time of his retirement after the 1988–89 season, Kareem held the NBA career records for most seasons, games, and minutes played; most points scored, field goals attempted and made, personal fouls and blocked shots. In 1980, he was named to the NBA's 35th Anniversary All-time Team. Kareem averaged 25 points per game during his NBA career, shot 56 percent from the floor, and pulled down more than 17,000 rebounds.

Off the court, Kareem is a very private person who devoutly practices the Islam religion, loves jazz, and peace and quiet. He is also intensely proud that the skinny kid from Manhattan has become a sports immortal.

Larry Joe Bird

"The Hick from French Lick"
December 7, 1956–

The marvelous thing about Larry Bird is that each year he improves. Although he has been one of the top players in the National Basketball Association since he joined the league in 1980, each season he finds a different part of his game to work on. Always a peerless passer and deadly shooter, in the later part of his career he improved his defensive play, particularly his ability to drop off the person he is covering to put pressure on the ballhandler or cut off the passing lanes. He also added the most accurate three-point shot in the game to his arsenal of shots. Larry's trademark, however, is his team play, hustle, and uncanny ability to make the big play when the game is on the line.

Bird hails from the small town of French Lick, Indiana, where he was a standout high school basketball player. He did not fit into Bobby Knight's program at Indiana University, so he transferred to little-known Indiana State in Terre Haute. State went 25–3 with Larry as a sophomore; 29–9 in

Larry Bird looks for the open man before driving to the basket. (Courtesy of the Boston Celtics.)

his junior year, and won 33 straight games in his senior year. That season, Larry won the College Player of the Year Award in every poll conducted, as he scored 28.7 points per game. Indiana State was finally stopped in the NCAA tournament by Michigan State, led by Earvin "Magic" Johnson.

Bird won the NBA's Rookie of the Year Award in 1980 and the league's Most Valuable Player Award in 1984, 1985 and 1986, and was selected the 1985 and 1986 playoffs' Most Valuable Player. Bird's Boston Celtics teams have won the league championship in 1981, 1984 and 1986 and the division title every year Bird has been on the team, except 1983, 1989 and 1990.

Since joining the National Basketball Association, Larry converted 50 percent of his shots from the floor and 87 percent from the foul line, as he averaged 24 points per game. An all-around player, he has always been among the league leaders in rebounds and assists. He was voted to the mid-season and post-season All-Star team each of his first eight years in the league. As league Most Valuable Player, Larry is in exclusive company,

Larry Bird takes one to the hoop for the Celtics. (Courtesy of Naismith Memorial Basketball Hall of Fame.)

having won the award three consecutive seasons, 1984, 1985, and 1986, a feat matched only by Wilt Chamberlain and Bill Russell.

In his first eight seasons with the Celtics, Larry has led the team in minutes played, field goals made, defensive rebounds, steals, points, and scoring average. This string was interrupted when Bird missed a large part of the 1988–89 season when he had both feet operated on. He returned in the fall of 1989 with his marvelous game still intact.

The 1985–86 season may have been Bird's best statistically as he finished near the top of the National Basketball Association in five key categories. He was first in free throw percentage, seventh in rebounding, and ninth in steals.

Larry Bird can do it all: score, pass, rebound, hustle, shoot fouls, lead, and play defense. But he does one thing better than any of the above — he wins.

James Nathaniel Brown

February 17, 1936–

Jim Brown got up slowly from the bottom of the pile and dragged himself back to the huddle. From the stands he appeared to be reeling and might need a few plays on the sidelines to clear the cobwebs from his head, and get some life back into his aching legs. The next play was designed to pick up three yards and a first down. The quarterback called Brown's number.

The play was simple: an inside trap, in which Jim hesitated for an instant until his right guard got his shoulder into the midsection of the opposing right tackle. The block was barely adequate, but was good enough for Brown to power through the line and burst into the secondary. Suddenly it was a foot race to the goal line between the bruising, 228-pound Brown and two smaller safeties. It was no contest; Brown scored untouched. He walked back to the bench like he had used every ounce of strength on that run and appeared to be finished for the afternoon. Brown scored twice more that day.

Jim Brown is generally considered to be the greatest running back to ever play football. In nine years in the National Football League, he carried the ball for 12,312 yards, averaging 5.2 yards per carry, and had 58 games in which he gained 100 yards or more. Jim was the first of the heavy duty runners who carried 30 to 35 times per game and ran both inside and outside.

Jimmy Brown was born on St. Simons Island, Georgia, and spent most of his early days with his grandmother and great-grandmother. When he was seven he joined his mother in Manhasset, Long Island, a New York City suburb, where she worked as a domestic. Jim was a tough kid who was headed in the wrong direction. He began hanging around with a bad element, even became a gang leader, but fortunately got into sports and found a healthy outlet for his energies. Jim starred in baseball, football, basketball, and lacrosse at Manhasset High School. Although lacrosse was considered his best sport, Brown once scored 55 points in a basketball game, a scholastic record for Long Island at that time. He was the finest football player on Long Island, and pitched and played first base for the varsity

Jim Brown at Syracuse University (Courtesy of Syracuse University).

baseball team. Brown went on to Syracuse University where he became a sports legend.

Jim won 10 letters in his three years of varsity competition at Syracuse (three in football, three in lacrosse, and two each in basketball and track and field) on his way to becoming an All-American in football and lacrosse. He became part of a tradition of outstanding running backs at Syracuse that includes Jim Nance, Ernie Davis, Floyd Lyttle, Larry Czonka, and Joe Morris. He ran for 2091 yards and scored 25 touchdowns in three seasons. Jim capped his college career by scoring 21 points in the Cotton Bowl as Syracuse lost to Texas Christian University, 28–27, on January 1, 1957.

Brown could have succeeded professionally in several sports. Although he was a sure thing to make the United States team, he passed up the opportunity to compete in the decathlon in the 1956 Olympics because of his commitment to the Syracuse football program. He later said, "It wouldn't be fair. I was in Syracuse on a football scholarship and the Olympics would have cut into the time I was committed to give to football." He also declined a lucrative offer from a Syracuse boxing promoter to pursue a career as a heavyweight boxer. Jim, however, never regretted selecting professional football as his avenue to sports immortality.

In 1957, Jim Brown was the first draft choice of the Cleveland Browns, a team that was 5–7 the previous year, and he led them to the National Football League's Eastern Division title in his rookie year. He established his reputation that season by gaining a record 237 yards in one game against the Los Angeles Rams on his way to becoming the league's leading rusher and its unanimous choice as Rookie of the Year. He improved the following season, setting the league record for 1507 yards rushing in 12 games, and scoring a record-tying 18 touchdowns. The United Press International named him Player of the Year and he won the Jim Thorpe Award as the league's Most Valuable Player for the first of two times. Brown was unsurpassed for durability and consistency. He led the league in rushing for eight of the nine seasons he played for the Browns, and for five years consecutively from 1957 through 1961. He gained over 1,000 yards in seven 12-game seasons and never missed a game, nor suffered a serious injury. Jim Brown set the standards by which running backs are measured.

Jimmy was one of the few athletes who retired at his peak to begin a new career in public relations and motion pictures. He had acted creditably in the movie *Rio Conchos* during his playing days, and became established in Hollywood with his role in *The Dirty Dozen*. Jim has had numerous acting roles and has promoted a variety of products. Still fit in his fifties, Brown continues to be a prominent public figure.

Today, when an exciting new running back breaks into professional football, old-time fans can be heard to say "He's good, but he's no Jim Brown."

Wilton Norman Chamberlain

"Wilt the Stilt," "The Big Dipper"
August 21, 1936–

The rookie center for the Philadelphia Warriors of the National Basketball Association was a hometown favorite. His press clippings said that he could play basketball better than anyone before him had. At 7 feet, 1 1/16 inches tall, the fans expected him to score every time he got his hands on the basketball. Wilt Chamberlain often did.

Wilt was the first basketball player over seven feet tall who could run, jump, shoot, and play defense as well as any other professional. His all-around game was so good that basketball changed radically because of him. Wilton Norman Chamberlain was born in the midst of the Great Depression in 1936 in Philadelphia. His father was a good provider and the nine Chamberlain children always had a roof over their heads and three square meals a day. As a youngster, Wilt collected and sold scrap, hawked papers, and carried groceries home for neighbors.

Wilt was 6'11" and still growing at age 13, so the local coaches required little imagination to visualize him in a basketball uniform. He led Philadelphia's Overbrook High School to national acclaim and may have been the finest high school basketball player of all time. Young Wilt was a scoring machine. He set a state record with 71 points as a freshman, broke it with 74 in his sophomore year, and registered 90 as a senior. College recruiters stood in line just to talk with Wilt.

Wilt chose the University of Kansas and accepted a basketball and track scholarship. Kansas' floundering basketball program came to life when Wilt joined the varsity squad in his sophomore year. In his first game, he shot 20 for 29 from the floor, scored 52 points, and came down with 31 rebounds as Kansas trounced a Northwestern team that was not ready to play basketball Chamberlain style. Kansas, a run-of-the-mill team before Chamberlain arrived, lost in triple overtime to Frank McGuire's undefeated North Carolina squad, 54–53, in the NCAA playoff finals. In that game, Wilt had 30 points, 19 rebounds and 9 blocked shots and proved that although he was only a sophomore, he was the best college basketball player in the nation.

Wilt's junior year was a disappointment. He and several of his teammates suffered a series of injuries and rival Kansas State earned the bid to the NCAA tourney for the Big 8. Only 8 teams were invited to the tournament in those days as postseason play was far more limited than today.

Wilt was not happy with the basketball program at Kansas and in his junior year opted to travel with the Harlem Globetrotters instead of completing his college career and education.

Wilt joined the Philadelphia Warriors in the fall of 1959 and made his regular-season debut at New York's Madison Square Garden. Professional basketball would never be the same after that night. Wilt scored 43 points against the New York Knickerbockers and retrieved 28 rebounds. These became normal figures for Chamberlain, who averaged 37.6 points and 26.9 rebounds per game in his rookie year, and took a mediocre Philadelphia team as far as the sixth game of the Eastern Division finals. Wilt was Rookie of the Year and the league's Most Valuable Player.

Wilt proceeded to become the most prolific scorer basketball had known. The numbers he attained can scarcely be believed by people who never saw him play.

In his second year, Chamberlain broke every NBA record he set in his first year and added another, shooting 50.5 percent from the field, the first time that had been done in the league. His third year was more prolific. He scored over 50 points 44 times and averaged 50.4 points per game for the season. That year he scored 100 points in one game against the New York Knickerbockers, a mark that has never been approached. His team lost to the Boston Celtics in the seventh game of the NBA finals.

Wilt starred on two of the greatest basketball teams of all time: the 1966–67 Philadelphia 76ers, who were 68–13, and the 1971–72 Los Angeles Lakers, who finished at 69–13.

In the latter part of his career Wilt concentrated more on defense and passing than on scoring, and he even led the league in assists. Every now and then, however, he would go out and score 50 or 60 points, just to let people know that he had not lost the touch.

Wilt was an all-around athlete and had the potential to excel in several sports. He won the Big 8 high-jump championship for Kansas in both his sophomore and junior years. He was an excellent quarter miler, turning in a 48-seconds-flat time in high school. Several times in his professional career he considered changing sports. He had serious professional football offers and almost signed for a heavyweight title bout against Muhammad Ali. Wilt was not merely tall; he was strong, agile, and fast.

Fans had a love/hate relationship with Wilt. He was not popular when he first broke into the NBA. Fans seemed to resent his height, skill, and swinging-bachelor image. In his legendary battles with his contemporary, Bill Russell, Wilt was viewed as Goliath against "little" Russell, who was only 6′ 9″. Russell's teams usually won; he had the likes of Cousy, Heinsohn, Sam and K.C. Jones, and Havlicek on his side throughout his career. Chamberlain usually won the battle in the middle and customarily outscored his popular opponent. After Wilt returned from a serious knee injury that sidelined him for most of the 1969–70 season, people appreciated his achievements more, and he became a hero to the Los Angeles sports fans.

Wilt was the NBA Most Valuable Player four times and won that award twice in the playoffs. He captained most of the teams he played on. His prolific scoring and rebounding records have never been approached in the entire history of basketball. He was an aggressive shot blocker, yet he never fouled out of an NBA game. He passed as well as any big man who ever played the game. No player has dominated a basketball era as has Wilt Chamberlain.

Tyrus Raymond Cobb

"The Georgia Peach"
December 18, 1886–July 18, 1961

He never won a popularity contest, but no one before him or since could put the round bat on the round ball as well as Ty Cobb. "Mean," "loner," "cantankerous," "opinionated," "ornery," and "a snarling wildcat," were some of the more polite terms used to describe Cobb. He delighted in the epithets; fan and press abuse drove him to peak performances. Ty Cobb loved to be hated.

Cobb had the finest batting eye in the history of baseball and a determination that bordered on the demonic. No one ran the bases more aggressively, some say "dirtier," than Cobb, nor did anyone take such fierce pride in forcing an opponent into a mental error.

Cobb's record lifetime batting average, .367 over 24 seasons, has stood unchallenged for more than 50 years and will be the highest lifetime average at the end of the 20th century. Cobb was so much better than his contemporaries that he led the American League in batting every year except one from 1907 through 1920. In 1916, his .371 average was only good enough for second place behind Tris Speaker's .386. Cobb was runner up again in batting in 1922 when his .401 could not match George Sisler's .420. Ty batted over .300 for 23 consecutive seasons.

Cobb simply did not strike out. His consistency in batting can be traced to his split-hand grip, in which he held the bat with his hands five inches apart. Cobb accepted the resulting loss of power because the grip enabled him to hit the ball wherever it was pitched.

Ty Cobb was a big man — six feet tall, 190 pounds — bigger than most players of his era, and he intimidated anyone who would give him an inch.

Opposite left: **Wilt Chamberlain when he was a dominant player at the University of Kansas (Courtesy of University of Kansas).** *Right:* **February 16, 1972: the night "Wilt the Stilt" scored his 30,000th point. (Courtesy of Naismith Basketball Hall of Fame.)**

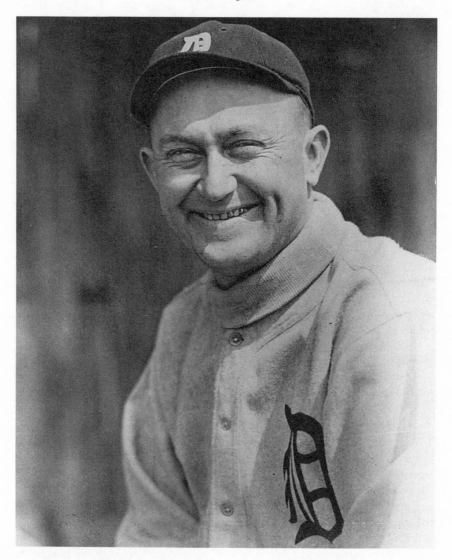

Tyrus Raymond Cobb in a Detroit Tiger uniform. (Courtesy National Baseball Library, Cooperstown, N.Y.)

After he retired, he enjoyed hearing stories of how he sharpened his spikes to remind opponents that he considered the base path his property. He record of 95 steals in a season held up for 47 years, and only two people have surpassed his lifetime total of 982 stolen bases. Cobb stole home 34 times. He thrived on taking an extra base on a hit or out-thinking an opponent to advance a runner or cause an error. He was the finest bunter ever,

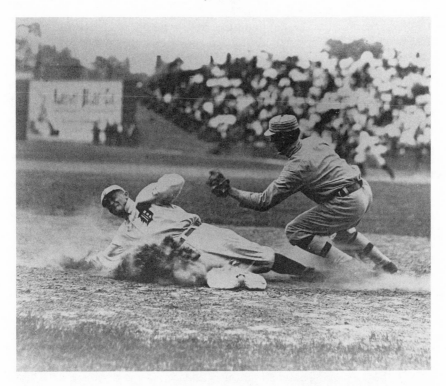

Cobb's all-out effort enables him to slide under "Home Run" Baker of Philadelphia's tag. (Courtesy National Baseball Library, Cooperstown, N.Y.)

and perfected the technique of faking a bunt to draw in an infielder, only to drive the ball past him. Cobb's ferocious base running antagonized opponents and their fans. One time, his high-flying spikes cut the arm of Home Run Baker, the Philadelphia Athletic's popular third baseman. When Cobb's Detroit Tigers next came to Philadelphia for a four-game series, tensions mounted. Thousands of fans shouted and jeered outside the Tigers' hotel. Ty required a police escort for the trip to the ball park. Ty counted 13 death threats that weekend, some of which the police took seriously. Three hundred extra policemen patrolled the park, looking for potential assassins. Boos echoed throughout the park as Ty took the field, and greeted him at each turn at bat. The Tigers won three of four in the series, and Ty batted safely in 18 of 28 appearances, collecting seven extra-base hits. Cobb thought that it was his greatest series.

Some modern critics think that Ty could not hit the long ball like today's players. Ty played when the ball was dead, the fences distant. He led the American League in home runs in 1909 with nine, fine production for that era before a cork center added life to the baseball during the 1920s. The trick pitches, such as the spit and shine ball, were phased out at the end of Cobb's career, and long-ball hitting became fashionable with the arrival of Babe Ruth.

In 1926, Ty's last season as an active player, he gave a hint of what he might have done if he had played in the live ball era. In one game in early May, Ty went five for six, hitting three home runs and a double. The next day, he hit two home runs and a single, not bad for a washed-up, old slap-hitter.

Although he was not as gifted an outfielder as he was a hitter, Cobb was a fine defensive ball player. He stretched average physical ability into excellent performances with hustle and intelligence. He compensated for a throwing arm injured in 1915, by playing shallow centerfield and consistently throwing to the correct base.

Cobb was born in Narrows, Georgia, the son of William Hershall Cobb, a well-known local figure who taught mathematics, was a school district superintendent, local newspaper editor, and state senator. Young Ty had a normal middle class upbringing and was expected to be a doctor or lawyer.

One personality trait stood out: Ty hated to lose. Old acquaintances tell of the time he beat up a chubby fifth-grade classmate when the poor lad's incorrect answer caused the boys' team to lose a spelling bee to the girls' team.

Ty began playing baseball seriously as a teenager and soon was the best player in town. He was surprised to receive his father's approval to play organized baseball, since players in those days were known to be rowdy and footloose. In his first year of professional ball, Ty was devastated by the news that his father was accidentally shot and killed by his mother who mistook him for a prowler. Ty became withdrawn, bitter, and belligerent, and he devoted all his energies to winning baseball games. Many people feel that he was driven by his father's last words to him when he left home for a baseball career, "Don't come home a failure."

Cobb had a sad retirement. He spent much of his time alone, frequently hunting, and soon boredom and alcohol dominated his life. His wife of 37 years divorced him, and he saw two of his six children die at the early ages of 33 and 41.

Cobb was noted for his confidence in his own ability and his contempt for modern ball players. At one Old-Timers game, shortly before his death, a newsman asked Ty what he thought he would hit against the current crop of pitchers. "Around .300, I guess," Cobb said with unaccustomed modesty. "C'mon, Ty," chided the newsman, "I'll bet you could hit better than that." "I'm not sure," Ty smiled, "You gotta remember that I'm over 71."

Mildred Ella Didrikson

"The Texas Babe"
June 26, 1911–September 27, 1956

She came storming out of Texas in 1930 with all the subtlety of a midwestern twister, sweeping away all the competition in sight. She played basketball for the Employers Casualty Insurance Company of Dallas and was an All-American her first three years out of high school. Her team won the National AAU basketball championship in 1931, and finished second in the national tournament in both 1930 and 1932. Basketball was a low-scoring game then, with a jump ball after every basket, no shot clock or fast break, and few personal fouls. A normal score was 25–19. In the five-game 1930 National AAU Tournament, Mildred Didrickson averaged 42 points per game . . . and basketball was not her best sport.

Mildred Ella Didrikson was the sixth of seven children born to Norwegian immigrants in Port Arthur, Texas. The family moved to Beaumont, Texas, after a hurricane and subsequent flooding wiped out its home and possessions. The South End of Beaumont was no place for sissies in those days. Mildred, a thin, strong young lady, learned to protect her turf and bloodied the nose of more than one lad who challenged it. By the time she was a high school junior, Mildred was the best female basketball player in the state of Texas. Halfway through her senior year, the Employer Casualty Insurance Company recruited her, officially as a typist, but more than incidentally as a forward on the company's basketball team. With Mildred on board, a very good team became the best in the nation.

Employers Casualty organized a women's track team in 1930 and Didrikson enthusiastically joined. Although she had no previous track experience, it was apparent that she was a natural in several events. Mildred loved the sport, and every day after work she practiced sprinting, shot putting, tossing the discus, and hurdling. Within a few months she was the best in Texas in virtually every women's track event, and on her way to stardom in a second sport.

Few athletes have ever had a more successful day than Mildred did on July 16, 1932. The Women's National AAU track championship and 1932 Olympic Trials were combined into one meet held at Dyche Stadium in Evanston, Illinois. The finest women's track teams in the country were assembled, including Employers Casualty Insurance, represented by one person, Mildred Didrikson. In the space of three hours, Didrikson compiled 30 points to win single-handedly the women's track championship of the United States. The Illinois Women's Athletic Club of Chicago finished second with 22 points.

Mildred entered eight events that day, won five outright, tied for first

Didrikson in 1950. (Courtesy of Lamar University.)

in a sixth, and placed fourth in a seventh. She was shut out in the eighth, when she failed to qualify for the final in the 100-yard dash. She set world records in the javelin throw, 80 meter hurdles, baseball throw, and high jump (in which she tied for first). She also won the long jump and shot put, and finished fourth in the discus.

Only five track events were held for women in the 1932 Olympics and the rules restricted individual participation to three. A disappointed Didrikson opted for the hurdles, javelin, and high jump. She headed for the first Los Angeles Olympics with a reputation as the finest woman athlete the United States had ever produced. International competition, although new to her, did not phase this Texan.

Mildred Didrikson won gold medals in the javelin and 80-meter hurdles, and received the silver medal in the high jump. She actually tied for first in the high jump, but was placed second on a technicality because of her innovative style; her head preceded her torso in clearing the crossbar. As usual, Mildred was decades ahead of her time.

Babe Didrikson excelled in swimming, diving, track and field, and golf. (Courtesy of Lamar University.)

Didrikson was proclaimed "The World's Greatest Woman Athlete" as a result of her Olympic performance. Because opportunities in professional sports were limited in the 1930s, particularly for women, Mildred earned a living giving exhibitions in a variety of sports. When sportswriters commented that she swung a bat like Babe Ruth, she earned the nickname "Babe." In the mid-1930s, Babe Didrikson played many exhibition games with major league baseball players and traveled with the legendary House of David, a bearded, barnstorming, professional team. She even tried vaudeville, boxing exhibitions, and played on coed basketball teams. In December of 1938 she married George Zaharias, a well-known professional wrestler and promoter. At this point in her career she decided to take up two sports which had well-established women's amateur competition, tennis and golf.

Babe's tennis career did not work out because she was declared a professional. She was allowed to play amateur golf only after sitting out several seasons to reestablish her amateur status. Babe soon became the finest woman golfer in the world. During 1946 and 1947 she won 17 consecutive tournaments, including the British Amateur, the first time that event was won by an American. She turned professional in 1948 and was to the women's tour what Arnold Palmer became to the men's tour. Babe won the United States Open in 1948 and 1950, was second in 1949 and finished third in 1951. She won the World's Championship Tournament in 1948, '49, '50, and '51, and was third in '52 and '53.

Babe Didrikson Zaharias was voted the Associated Press' Woman Athlete of the Year six times, and in 1950 was chosen the Greatest Female Athlete of the First Half of the 20th Century.

Babe was struck with cancer in 1953, but rallied to win the World Championship Golf Tournament in 1954. She lost her battle to cancer in September of 1956, at the age of 45.

Don't be fooled the next time a trivia buff asks you to name the only person to win two Olympic gold medals and the United States Open in golf. Just tell him her name was Mildred.

Joseph Paul DiMaggio

"Joltin' Joe," "The Yankee Clipper"
November 25, 1914–

The shy young rookie from San Francisco lost little time in making an impact in the major leagues. Joe DiMaggio joined a Yankees team that was floundering. Babe Ruth was gone and Lou Gehrig, as good as he was, could not carry the entire franchise. The Ruth-Gehrig Yankees had won in 1927, 1928, and 1932, but Connie Mack's Philadelphia Athletics, led by Lefty Grove, Jimmy Foxx, and Al Simmons, had won the American League pennant in 1929, '30, and '31. The Yankees squeezed in in 1932, but Washington in 1933 and Detroit in '34 and '35 were the class of the American League. The California kid was all the Yankees needed to make their 1936 edition one of the finest three or four baseball teams ever assembled.

When Joe DiMaggio broke into the 1936 Yankee lineup, he was so shy that newsmen wondered whether or not he could speak. But Joe let his performance do his talking, and it was soon apparent that he could throw, field, hit, and run with anyone playing the game.

Those '36 Yankees won the American League pennant by 19½ games and went on to sweep the World Series. DiMaggio batted .323, hit 29 home runs, 15 triples, 44 doubles, and batted in 125 runs. Even as a rookie his fielding was compared with Bob Meusel and Tris Speaker, the premier outfielders who preceded Joe. Baserunners challenged his rookie arm, allowing DiMaggio to lead the American League with 22 outfield assists. After that they learned. Even at the end of his playing career, when there was nothing left of his fine throwing arm, base runners stayed put when the ball was hit to DiMaggio.

Joe came from a family of Italian fishermen. He disliked the fisherman's life and avoided getting up early and going out for the daily catch whenever possible. But the DiMaggios found time to play baseball, and Joe and his brothers learned to play well. Older brother Vince had a 10-year National League career as a regular for Boston, Pittsburgh, and Philadelphia. Dominic, the youngest of the DiMaggios, starred for the Boston Red Sox for 11 years, compiling a .298 lifetime batting average while rivaling Joe as a centerfielder. Joe always insisted that his oldest brother, Tom, was the best ballplayer in the family, but he did not have the opportunity to play the game professionally.

DiMaggio's career was brief compared with most superstars. He played on 13 major league seasons, yet his teams won the American League pennant ten times and the World Series nine. He lost three full seasons to military service and half of another to injuries. Joe consistently played in pain from elbow, shoulder, and heel injuries. DiMaggio will always be remembered for his 56-game hitting streak in 1941. Joe's streak became the talk of the country. Pressure mounted as he surpassed George Sisler's modern major-league record of 41 games, and Wee Willie Keeler's 1887 mark of 44. The United States, on the verge of World War II, took DiMaggio and his streak to heart as he continued to hit in game after game. Finally, he was stopped in Cleveland by two great backhanded stops by Indian third baseman, Kenny Keltner, as he went 0 for 3 with a walk. A hit song of the era summed up the fans' reaction to his playing with this refrain:

"Joltin' Joe DiMaggio ... we want you on our side."

After that game in Cleveland, Joe continued to hit in 16 more games consecutively.

Hitting streaks were nothing new to Joltin' Joe, who had hit in 61 straight games for the 1933 San Francisco Seals of the Triple A Pacific Coast League. Because he was frequently injured, DiMaggio's career was highlighted by a series of dramatic comebacks including his performance in a late June 1949 series in Boston's Fenway Park. Operations for crippling bone spurs, first on the left heel and then on the right, seemed to have ended his career before the 1949 season began. At the close of June a gutsy Yankee team still led the American League, but the fast-closing Red Sox had

DiMaggio connects for a home run in the fifth and last game of the 1949 World Series against the Brooklyn Dodgers. (National Baseball Library, Cooperstown, N.Y.)

won 10 of their last 11 games. The stage was set for the return of Di-Maggio.

In that series, Joe's first of the season, the Yankees won the first game, 5–4, and Joe had two hits, including a two-run homer. The Yanks spotted the Red Sox a 7–1 lead in the second game until Joe got going. His three-run homer made it 7–4, and his second home run of the day won the game 8–7. The Yankees completed the sweep the next day when DiMaggio hit another game-winning homer. That year, the Yanks beat Boston on the last day of the season, and went on to defeat the Dodgers in the World Series.

DiMaggio's lifetime batting average was .325, and he won back-to-back batting titles in 1939 and 1940, with averages of .381 and .352. Joe also had two home run titles with 46 in 1936 and 39 in 1948, quite a feat for a right-handed batter in Yankee Stadium, famous for its Death Valley in left and center fields. But Joe's contributions are not measured in statistics; he was probably the most graceful outfielder in baseball history. His courage in overcoming painful injuries inspired his teammates in an era when the Yankees were virtually unbeatable. He was the American League's Most Valuable Player in 1939, 1941, and 1947. For 13 years he was as inspiring a leader as any team has had.

Most modern sluggers strike out four or five times for every home run they hit. DiMaggio hit 363 career home runs and struck out only 369 times, an average of 28 strikeouts per season, or one strikeout in every 21 at bats.

Joe is a legend; to many fans the last of the athletic heroes. His class on and off the field has gained him universal respect.

Wayne Gretzky
"The Great One"
Jan. 26, 1961–

Wayne Gretzky is so good that most experts accepted him as the finest hockey player of all time before his 25th birthday. Many, in fact, believe that he had earned that reputation before he was 21.

Wayne was not born wearing skates, but soon after he could walk his father had him skating on a makeshift rink in their backyard in Brantford, Ontario. He was in a class by himself in age-group hockey, and scored 378 goals in 85 games when he was 10. As a teenager he worked his way up through the junior hockey leagues, and in July 1978, at the age of 17, signed with the Indianapolis Racers of the World Hockey Association. His contract was soon bought by the Edmonton Oilers because the Racers played before too many empty seats.

Many North Americans, who previously had only a vague idea where Edmonton was, began to recognize that city as the hockey capital of the world. After Wayne played one season in the World Hockey Association, the owners of the National Hockey League realized his drawing potential, and the 18-year-old became the primary force for merging the two leagues. No one was disappointed with the results. Gretzky had a sensational first

Wayne Gretzky stickhandles around Tomas Sandstrom of the New York Rangers, looking to set up an Oiler teammate. (Courtesy of Bruce Bennett.)

year in the National Hockey League, scoring 51 goals and adding 86 assists for 137 points, leading the league in points and goals. He won the Hart Trophy for scoring, the Lady Byng for sportsmanship and performance, and was a first-string all-star. Wayne was just getting used to NHL play.

Gretzky won the Ross Trophy as the league's Most Valuable Player eight consecutive years, from 1980 through 1987. He also won the scoring title each of those years and led the league in assists every year from 1981 through 1987. In 1986, he scored 214 points on 52 goals and an incredible 162 assists. He has been a first team all-star in every one of his NHL seasons. Hockey fans coined the expression BILBG (Best in League Besides Gretzky).

Despite his scoring and assist accomplishments, Wayne is best known for his all-around team performance. His first four years in the league saw the New York Islanders win the Stanley Cup. The Oilers improved each year and finished as high as second in 1983, but Wayne and his teammates were unable to bring the battered old Stanley Cup back to Alberta Province. The Oilers reached the top in 1984 when they defeated the Islanders to initiate a new dynasty. Gretzky and company repeated in 1985 with

Wayne winning the Conn Smythe Award as Most Valuable Player in the playoffs.

Wayne Gretzky's career highlights from his NHL rookie year until his trade to the Los Angeles Kings before the 1988–1989 season look like this:

Hart Trophy (League MVP)	Art Ross Trophy (Scoring Leader)	Conn Smythe (Playoff MVP)	Lester Pearson (Players' MVP)
1980			
1981	1981		
1982	1982		1982
1983	1983		1983
1984	1984		1984
1985	1985	1985	1985
1986	1986		
1987	1987		1987
		1988	

Gretzky won the World Hockey League's Rookie of the Year in 1979, the NHL's Lady Byng Award as its most gentlemanly player in 1980, and the Emery Edge Award for the best plus/minus statistics in 1984, 1985, and 1987.

Wayne Gretzky had an off-year in 1988 when injuries forced him to miss a large part of the season. Yet in 64 games he scored 40 goals and had 109 assists, for a most acceptable total of 149 points. That season also marked the emergence of Mario Lemieux, the youngster of the Pittsburgh Penguins whose scoring feats topped the "old man," 27-year-old Gretzky, for that season. Yet Wayne was sound for the playoffs, and led Edmonton to the Stanley Cup. Wayne scored 12 goals and had 31 assists in 19 games during the playoffs to win the MVP Award.

On August 10, 1988, an era ended in Canada when Wayne Gretzky, along with two players, was traded to the Los Angeles Kings for two players, three draft choices, and an estimated 10 million dollars. Wayne instantly made the Kings a playoff contender as he registered another MVP season in 1988–89. During the season, the 28-year-old Gretzky broke Gordie Howe's record of 1,850 points in a career. Gretzky did it in 780 games; it took Gordie 1767. Yet the game has changed. As Wayne said, "Gordie's still the greatest in my mind and the greatest in everyone else's mind." Maybe, but the L.A. King may be the new king.

Wayne has virtually rewritten the record book since he entered the league. Some of his more significant records are:

Most goals in a season	92	(1981–82)
Most assists in a season	163	(1985–86)
Most points in a season	215	(1985–86)
Most assists – playoffs	31	(1988)
Most points – playoff	47	(1985)
Most 100-point seasons	9	(consecutive)

In 1983–84, Gretzky assisted in 17 and scored in 51 straight games. By the start of the 1988–89 season, Wayne had 43 hat tricks (three or more goals in a game) and performed that feat ten times during the 1981–82 season.

In nine years of Stanley Cup play, Wayne has scored 81 goals and assisted 169 times for 250 points in 119 games. His closest competitor in this regard is Jean Beliveau, who scored 176 points in 162 games.

Wayne was the first Canadian, and first hockey player, to be named the *Sporting News* Man of the Year, and in 1982, he won Canada's Athlete of the Year Award for the first time.

Wayne Gretzky does more things well than any hockey player who preceded him. His puck handling, passing, shot making, and endurance are all outstanding, and his fine conditioning has enabled him to avoid serious injury despite his slight 5-11, 165-pound frame. There are few people who will question that he is the greatest hockey player of all time.

Gordon Howe
March 31, 1928–

Gordie Howe retired from the National Hockey League in 1971 with a performance and endurance record difficult to match in any sport. His 786 career goals were 232 more than runner-up Bobby Hull. He held the National Hockey League record for most games played, most seasons played, most asissts and most points. In 1972 he was elected to the Hockey Hall of Fame . . . and two years later, at age 45, he made a comeback. Howe then played professionally for nearly another decade.

Gordon Howe's professional hockey career extended from 1945, when he signed his first contract with the Omaha Knights, a Detroit Red Wing farm club, until 1980 when he finally retired from the Hartford Whalers, a span of close to 40 years. No professional athlete in any contact sport has ever come close to this achievement. When he broke into the six-team National Hockey League, Maurice Richard was a young star with the Montreal Canadians. When he retired, Wayne Gretzky had already established himself as the premier player in the game. Howe played 32 seasons of major-league hockey and appeared in the playoffs 26 times. In 2,421 games, he scored 1,071 points and totaled 2,589 points.

Gordon was born in Floral, Saskatchewan, and moved to Saskatoon as a youngster. Raised in a family of nine during the Great Depression, Gordie left school during his first year of high school to help support the family by doing construction work. Within a few years, his once skinny frame filled out to a rock hard six-feet, 205 pounds.

Gordie Howe was a grandfather in his fifties when he ended his career with the Hartford Whalers. (Courtesy of the Hartford Whalers.)

Gordie was no child star; in fact, he was a relatively ineffective goaltender as a youngster. Only when he matured and moved to wing did scouts begin to notice him. The New York Rangers let him get away from a tryout camp, but the Red Wings got his name on a contract and within two years, the 18 year old was playing in the National Hockey League. The Red Wings had been also-rans before Howe arrived in Detroit. While Howe played there, the Wings won nine league titles and four Stanley Cups. Since he left Detroit in 1971, the Wings have never been in the final round of Stanley Cup play. Howe was an ordinary player in his first few years in the NHL, but in the 1949–50 season he began producing superstar statistics. That season he scored 68 points with 35 goals and 33 assists. He teamed with Ted Linsey and Sid Abel to form "the Production Line," one of the finest in hockey history, and led Detroit to seven consecutive season championships. Gordie won the Hart Trophy as the league's Most Valuable Player six times, in 1952, '53, '57, '58, '60, and '63, and the Art Ross scoring trophy six times also in 1951, '52, '53, '54, '57, and '63. He was a first or second team all-star 21 times.

Howe had to overcome serious injury to stay on top. Brain surgery saved his life in 1950 when his skull was fractured by a check from Toronto's Ted Kennedy during Stanley Cup play. He later fractured his skull, cheekbone and nose in another hockey mishap, had both knees operated on, suffered numerous dislocations and broken bones, and required more than 300 stitches to hold parts of his body together. Yet, but for the one game he missed during the 1966–67 season he would have played in 690 consecutive games, sixty more than the existing endurance record. He accomplished this while playing an average of 45 minutes per game, twice the ice time of a normal wing.

Howe earned the reputation as one of the toughest fighters in the league and has added the scalp of more than one bad man to his collection. Yet Gordie has always been one of hockey's most popular players, both with the fans and his fellow players, and is known for his quiet, gentlemanly demeanor off the ice.

Howe never made more than $100,000 a season in his heyday so the lure of a million-dollar contract with the Houston Aeros of the World Hockey Association, and the opportunity to play with his sons, Mark and Marty, was too much to resist. Gordon played six seasons in the World Hockey League from 1973 through 1979. During this stretch of his career, Howe averaged 70 games, 29 goals, 56 assists, and 85 points per season. The Howes eventually moved to Hartford to play for the Whalers during the 1979–80 season. Howe was still an active player, a grandfather in his fifties, when the Whalers joined the National Hockey League as a result of the 1980 merger. He was no bit player in his last season, appearing in all 80 games Hartford played, and accumulating 41 points.

Gordie Howe finally retired after the 1980 season, this time for keeps, at the age of 52. Howe's skill, determination, and durability make him one of the legends of 20th century sports.

Joe Louis

Born: Joseph Louis Barrow
May 13, 1914–April 12, 1981

Joe Louis was a menacing sight in the ring, stalking an opponent and looking for the opening through which he could unleash the awesome power loaded in both his fists. Six-feet, 1½ inches tall, and an even 200 pounds in his prime, Joe bore in behind a devastating left jab, considered by many boxing experts to be the best jab any heavyweight possessed. It was not the flicking stab, the feather duster, that most boxers use to keep an opponent off balance; it was more of a battering ram that broke through an opponent's defenses and landed with a perceptible thud. The jab did not sting, it hurt, but it was only the calling card for the dynamite right that put many a fine heavyweight down for the count.

Many feel that Joe Louis was the perfect fighting machine: a heavy hitter, nimble and courageous, with a style that relentlessly pursued an opponent, constantly reducing the ring space in which he could maneuver. Joe's summary of this style was, "They can run, but they can't hide."

Joe Louis was a fighting champion, virtually unbeatable in his prime. From 1934 until 1948, the first 14 years of his career, he lost only once, a defeat he dramatically avenged.

Louis was born Joseph Louis Barrow, the son of an Alabama sharecropper. When he was 12 his mother moved the family to Detroit, where she hoped Joe would receive an education. She even used some of her hard-earned money for Joe's violin lessons, but the concert stage was not his destiny. Joe never advanced beyond the fifth grade and began hanging around the streets, occasionally delivering ice, when a friend invited him to the Brewster Street Recreation Center to join its boxing program. He was soon not only the best boxer at the club, but the best in Detroit. As a 20 year old, in 1934, he won the Golden Gloves heavyweight championship and turned professional, shortening his name to Joe Louis. He won 12 bouts within a year and earned his first big payday in New York's Yankee Stadium against Primo Carnara. Carnara was counted out in six rounds after absorbing a terrible beating. Three months later it took Joe only three rounds to dispose of another former heavyweight champion, Max Baer.

In 1936, Louis' relentless march toward the world's title was sidetracked by another former champion, Max Schmeling, who knocked Louis

Joe Louis in 1937. (Courtesy of AP/Wide World Photos.)

out in 12 rounds. Ironically the reigning heavyweight champion, Jim Braddock, elected to defend his title against Louis instead of Schmeling, the
more logical contender. Braddock seemed to have made a good choice
when Louis went down in the early rounds, but once he got going, Louis
easily knocked out Braddock to become undisputed heavyweight champion.

Louis' reputation as a fighting champion earned him universal respect.
Although Louis was champion a full decade before Jackie Robinson broke
the color line in organized baseball, most Americans, black or white, found
themselves rooting for the popular black man from Detroit.

Louis' two greatest fights were his return match with Max Schmeling,
whom he battered senseless in less than one round, and his 13-round
knockout of the classic boxer and light-heavyweight champion, Billy Conn.
In that bout, Conn was ahead after 12 rounds, 7–5, 7–4–1, on two judges'
cards, and even on the third, but he made the fatal mistake of trying to put
Joe Louis away in the 13th by slugging it out toe-to-toe with him. Conn was
counted out with 2 seconds left in the round.

Prior to the Conn fight, Louis defeated every possible heavyweight

Joe Louis sends Max Schmeling to the canvas for keeps in the first round of their 1938 rematch. (Courtesy of AP/Wide World Photos.)

contender. In one streak in 1939 and 1940, he defended his title six times within six months, a feat which some critics labelled the "Bum of the Month Club."

After one more title defense, Louis entered the service for a four-year hitch during World War II. He had little of his prewar skill left when he returned to the ring from the service, yet he easily defeated Conn again and defended his crown twice against Jersey Joe Walcott. Joe knew it was time to quit after the second Walcott bout in June 1948, and retired from the ring, vacating his title.

Joe Louis knew little about handling money and his managers, both of whom had gambling backgrounds, made no provision for Joe's retirement. By 1950, Joe was back in the ring trying to pay off a large tax liability owed to the United States government in the only way he knew how, with his fists. He lost a 15-round title bid to champion Ezzard Charles, and was devastated by a promising young heavyweight, Rocky Marciano.

Joe was in debt for his remaining years. He wrestled professionally briefly, did some refereeing, and made public appearances for expense money. He became a greeter at the hotels and casinos in Las Vegas. But his reputation never diminished. Everyone loved Joe Louis, probably the greatest heavyweight champion of the century.

Christopher Mathewson

"Christy"
August 12, 1880–October 7, 1925

The monument in the "holy of holies" at Cooperstown, New York, where baseball people worship, reads:

> Christy Mathewson . . . greatest of all the great pitchers of the 20th century's first quarter. Pitched 3 shutouts in the 1905 World Series. First pitcher of the century ever to win 30 games in 3 consecutive years. Won 37 games in 1908.

But the monument tells only part of the story.

Christy Mathewson was born on August 12, 1880, in Factoryville, Pennsylvania, to Christopher and Minerva Mathewson. Christy's parents were prosperous and well-educated, and provided him with a fine education at Bucknell University. He starred in three sports, baseball, football, and basketball, pitched semiprofessionally for the local Honesdale baseball team, and still found time to be elected class president, play in the college band, sing in the glee club, be a member of two fraternities and the Eupian Literary Society. No one ever recorded whether or not Christy swept the gymnasium after practice. Mathewson was so good at football that Walter Camp named him to his 12-man All-American team in 1900 as its kicker.

Matty learned to throw a screwball (he called it a fadeaway) in the minors, and by the time he made the major leagues, he could put it exactly where he wanted to.

The year 1901 marked his third and last year at Bucknell and the beginning of one of the finest careers in the history of major league baseball. The New York Giants were a terrible team at the turn of the century, finishing last in 1900 and 1902, and next to last in 1901. Mathewson was 20-17 with the 1901 edition. That year he had a 2.41 earned run average, a no-hitter against St. Louis in July, and two two-hitters. So inept was Giant management that it decided to convert Christy to a first baseman/outfielder during the 1902 season. Fortunately for Mathewson and the Giants, the great John McGraw was hired as manager in midseason and began to build one of baseball's finest dynasties by returning Christy to the mound. New York's original M and M boys, McGraw and Mathewson, brought that city its first popular sports team.

Matty was 14-17 with a 2.11 earned run average on a last-place team, but 8 of his 14 wins were shutouts. It was the last time the Giants would see the second division as long as Mathewson pitched for them.

From 1903 through 1914, Christy Mathewson was the finest pitcher baseball had known. He won 20 or more games for 12 consecutive seasons, a mark unequaled in the 20th century, and 30 or more four times, including three consecutively from 1903 through 1905.

In 1903 Matty was 30-13, with 37 complete games and 267 strikeouts. The following year Matty was 33-12, with a 2.03 earned run average. He started 46 games, completed 35 of them, and struck out a league-leading 212 batters. Mathewson even made two relief appearances and won both games.

The 1905 Giants won 105 games on their way to the National League pennant with Mathewson compiling a 31-8 record, which included his second no-hitter, and an incredible 1.27 earned run average. This time the Giants met Connie Mack's Philadelphia Athletics in the World Series and Mathewson and "Iron Man" McGinnity showed the upstarts why pitching is the name of the game. In fact, Christy's pitching performance was the finest ever in World Series history.

On October 9, 1905, Mathewson shut out the Athletics, 3-0, on four hits in the Series opener. McGinnity lost the next day by the same 3-0 score. A rain delay pushed the third game back to the 12th and allowed Mathewson to return with two days' rest. He shut out the A's 9-0 on four hits. On the 13th McGinnity tossed a five-hit shutout and nipped the A's 1-0. Mathewson then returned with one day's rest and again shut out the A's, this time 2-0 on six hits. Matty's totals for the Series were:

W	L	ERA	IP	H	BB	SO
3	0	0.00	27	14	1	18

Matty hit a batter and allowed one runner to reach third base in pitching his three consecutive shutouts.

At this point in his career, Christy had become America's first sports idol. An educated man in an era when baseball players were stereotyped as either hayseeds from the country whose only pair of shoes had spikes on them, or hard-drinking, profane, city toughs, Matty was idolized by sports fans and the general public. Mathewson was tall, strong and handsome, and loved by everyone who ever knew him. He was a devoted family man and smoked, drank, and cussed only on rare occasions.

Mathewson accomplished what many consider the finest pitching season ever accomplished by a pitcher in 1908. He was 37-11, appeared in 56 games, pitched 391 innings, had an ERA of 1.43 and saved five games. Ironically, it was the year that brought Mathewson his greatest disappointments.

Christy Mathewson warming up as he prepares to take to the mound at New York's Polo Grounds. (Courtesy of National Baseball Museum, Cooperstown, N.Y.)

On September 23, 1908, Mathewson ended up with a no-decision against arch-rival Chicago in one of baseball's most famous games, when teammate Fred Merkle mistakenly ran to the clubhouse from first base instead of running to second base when Al Bridwell hit what appeared to be a game-winning single. The teams subsequently tied at season's end and, of course, Mathewson was selected to pitch the playoff game, despite having already pitched over 390 innings that season. Mathewson lost, but made no excuses.

As good as he was in 1908, 1909 may have been his best year statistically. Matty won 25 and lost 6, with an ERA of 1.14.

Mathewson's statistics compare favorably with any pitcher of this century. He won 373 games and lost 188. His 373 wins ties him for third place on the all-time list with Grover Alexander and behind Walter Johnson's 416 and Cy Young's 508. Young won 255 of his games in the 19th century. Matty leads Young in winning percentage, .655 to .642, and in career earned run average, 2.13 to 2.56. Johnson, with his 416 wins, is 66 points behind Mathewson in winning percentage and is just behind Christy, 2.13 to 2.17, in lifetime ERA. Walter had four more seasons in the major leagues than Matty. From 1901, his first full season in the majors, until 1914, his last effective year, Christy Mathewson averaged 26 wins and 12 losses per season.

Mathewson had an excellent strikeout pitch and walked practically no one. He led the National League in strikeouts five times with a career best of 267 in 1903. He walked 100 batters that year, his highest total in the majors, but with a 30-13 record and a 2.26 ERA, the walks hurt him very little. During the 1913 and 1914 seasons, when his career was near its end, he walked a total of 44 men in 618 innings while winning 49 games. Mathewson pitched an entire month in 1913, 68 consecutive innings, without walking a batter. Yet Mathewson's arm was gone in 1915, and he retired in 1916 at the age of 35. During his career Mathewson walked only 846 batters while striking out 2,511, an average of 1.6 walks and 4.8 strikeouts per game.

Mathewson's career totals are:

YRS	W	L	pct.	ERA	IP	H	BB	SO	ShO	SV
17	373	188	.665	2.13	4783	4612	846	2511	83	27

And in World Series play, he was:

4	5	5	.500	1.15	101	76	10	48	4	0

After retiring as an active player from the Giants in 1916, Mathewson managed the Cincinnati Reds until he volunteered for army service in 1918. Christy, serving as a captain in the Army in France, was accidentally exposed to poison gas. Mathewson contracted tuberculosis in 1921 as a result and was given six months to live. He beat those odds to return to baseball as the general manager of the Boston Braves in 1923. The respiratory condition worsened, however, and Christy Mathewson died at a rest home in Saranac Lake, New York, in 1925, at the tragically young age of 45.

Grantland Rice, the noted sports columnist, wrote in Mathewson's obituary:

> There have been others who had as great an arm, others as much nerve, and probably a few just as smart, but when it comes to a combination of all these things, there will never be another Matty. Christy Mathewson brought something to baseball that no one else has ever given to the game. He handed the game a certain touch of class, an indefinable lift in culture, brains, and personality.

The last sentence on his monument at Cooperstown completes the story and summarizes how good a pitcher Christy Mathewson was. It reads "Matty was master of them all."

Willie Howard Mays

"Say Hey Kid"
May 6, 1931–

Major-league baseball scouts evaluate non-pitchers in five categories: running, catching, hitting for distance, hitting for average, and throwing. Willie Mays is one of the few players in the history of baseball who excelled in each category.

Willie's father was a railroad porter, and later a steelworker, in Birmingham, Alabama, and a semiprofessional center-fielder who played in the local industrial leagues. He never had the opportunity to play organized baseball. His son matured just after Jackie Robinson had opened the game to black players, and Willie's father saw the chance for his talented son to avoid a life slaving in the steel mills. Willie played basketball and football in high school (his school did not have a baseball team) and signed to play with the Birmingham Black Barons as a utility infielder in 1948, when he was a 16-year-old high school senior. Two years later, the New York Giants recruited him for their organization and he made the leap to major-league baseball in a little over one season. The Giants originally placed Willie at their minor-league affiliate in Trenton, New Jersey, and he played solidly there. The next season, 1951, Mays was promoted to the Minneapolis Millers, a Triple-A team. Willie was batting .477 with the Millers in mid–May when he received the call from Leo Durocher to play for the Giants at the Polo Grounds.

That season, 1951, the New York Giants were going nowhere. The

The "Say Hey Kid" is congratulated by his teammates after his seventh-game home run wins the 1954 World Series against the rival Brooklyn Dodgers.

proud champions of the John McGraw era had developed into a team that could hit home runs but could not win pennants. The 1951 edition seemed destined for a boring, nonproductive season until Mays arrived.

Willie's first home run was a milestone in New York sports history. After a few games of swinging through major-league curve balls, Willie's bat met squarely with one of Warren Spahn's fastballs and the ball cleared the Polo Grounds' double-deck left field grandstands as it was still climbing. But the fascinating thing about Mays is that although he hit some 660 home runs, people who saw him play always talk about his fielding.

In Mays' first month in the majors, Rocky Nelson, a Pittsburgh Pirates journeyman ball player, drove one off Giants' pitching to deep left-center in Forbes Field. Mays was off with the crack of the bat and almost caught up with the ball, but he could not get his gloved hand across his body to make the catch. Instead, the rookie snatched the ball out of the air with his bare right hand to make a catch that Leo Durocher talked about for years.

Wes Westrum, the veteran catcher and eventual manager of the New York Mets, tells this story about the rookie Mays. In August, the Giants and the hated Dodgers were locked in a tie game in the top of the eighth inning, with Billy Cox on third base for the Dodgers with one out. A drive to deep right-center field was tracked down by Mays in a spot where normally the runner's scoring from third base is conceded. Mays made the catch on the run, spun all the way around, and threw to home. "It was still going 85 miles per hour when I caught it," says Westrum, a person who made a career catching thrown balls. Cox was out by ten feet. Westrum added, "And any umpire in the majors would have called it a strike."

The Giants won their miracle pennant in 1951, when Bobby Thomson hit his famous home run as rookie Mays watched from the on deck circle.

Mays spent most of the 1952 and 1953 seasons in the armed forces during the Korean War, but returned to lead the New York Giants to the National League pennant again in 1954, and win the first of his two Most Valuable Player awards. Willie hit .345 that season, had 41 home runs, and drove in 110 runs. He led the league in triples with 13, and in slugging percentage. *The Sporting News* named him Player of the Year and he was awarded the Hickock Belt as the Professional Athlete of the Year.

Willie's most famous play occurred during the 1954 World Series when he turned his back on Vic Wertz of Cleveland's towering, 460-foot drive to center field, ran to the spot where it would descend, made an over-the-head catch running at full speed, and spun and threw a bullet back to the infield to hold a Cleveland runner on first base. The Giants eventually won that game on a Dusty Rhodes home run.

Only ten players in baseball have hit fifty or more home runs in a season. Some who did not reach this plateau include Lou Gehrig, Ted Williams, Hank Aaron, Reggie Jackson, Harmon Killerbrew and Joe DiMaggio. Five of the ten who have hit fifty in a season did it only once. Willie Mays, Ralph Kiner, Jimmy Foxx, and Mickey Mantle did it twice, and Willie had seasons where he hit 40, 49, and 47 home runs. Babe Ruth hit more than 50 in four seasons.

Willie was a great favorite with the fans. His image was enhanced when the newspapers mentioned that Willie was often seen playing stickball with the kids on the streets of Harlem, a few blocks from the Polo Grounds. They knew him as the "Say Hey Kid" then, a nickname he earned because he did not easily remember people's names and greeted them by saying "Say Hey." Willie was a happy man, exuberant, uninhibited, free-wheeling. New York loved him. Unfortunately for New York, the Giants moved to San Francisco in 1957, and Willie's magic was seen regularly in Seals' Stadium originally, and subsequently, Candlestick Park. The San Francisco fans took at least half a decade to take Mays to their hearts, and by that time he had established himself as one of the greatest baseball players of all time.

Mays was a marvel of consistency. During one stretch in his career, he scored 100 or more runs for 12 consecutive seasons and batted in more than

100 eight straight times. From 1954 through 1965, his batting average dipped below .300 twice, to .296 in both 1956 and 1964. He played in every All-Star game from 1954 until 1973.

Mays is still a favorite of the fans when they see him in Atlantic City where he works as a greeter at the casinos and at his frequent guest appearances. They remember his performances with fondness. After all, Willie was the finest baseball player during the second half of the 20th century.

Jack William Nicklaus

"The Golden Bear"
January 21, 1940–

He started the final round on that sunny April Sunday in Augusta in a seven-way tie for ninth, four strokes off the pace. Ahead of him in the quest for the green jacket, the symbol of supremacy in the 1986 Masters Golf Tournament, were the finest golfers in the world: Greg Norman, the "White Shark" from Australia, in the lead, followed by West Germany's Bernhard Langer, the defending champion, Seve Ballesteros, a two-time winner from Spain, South Africa's Nick Price, two great Americans, Tom Kite and Tom Watson, and Japan's Tommy Nakajima.

Jack Nicklaus had played poorly all year but the week before the Masters his game showed some signs of life. He began the tournament slowly but improved steadily, as he carded rounds of 74, 71, and 69. Jack told himself that he needed a final round of 65 to win, but at age 46, and not having won a major tournament in six years, chances were slim. Jack tightened the belt on his blue and white checkered trousers at the first tee and drove the ball 285 yards down the middle of the fairway. He played steadily on the front nine, finishing in 35 strokes. Jack's putter then got hot and he proceeded to tear up the revered back nine at Augusta with a seven-under-par 30, making him the leader in the clubhouse.

The great professionals still on the course each had his shot at Jack, but one by one they faltered. Watson never got a rally going, Kite missed a putt by an inch, Ballesteros found water, Norman, the gallery. The finest Master of them all had his most satisfying win in an unparalleled career with this, his sixth Augusta win.

Nicklaus' record speaks for itself; he is the greatest golfer who has ever played the game. He is the only person to win each of the "Big Four" golf tournaments three times, the British and United States opens, Professional Golfers Association (PGA) and the Masters.

As a youngster growing up in Columbus, Ohio, Nicklaus was an all-

Young Jack Nicklaus displayed perfect form and a powerful body even in his amateur days at Ohio State. (Courtesy of Ohio State University Archives.)

around athlete, excelling in football and basketball, and even despite his chubby appearance, in track. Jack gave up football in high school because it conflicted with his golf schedule, but he averaged 17.5 and 18.0 points per game in his last two high school basketball seasons. Jack could concentrate even then. He was a 90 percent foul shooter who once connected on 26 consecutive free throws.

When Jack was ten he took up golf at the urging of his father, a local pharmacist, and scored a 51 for nine holes in his first round. He broke 80 for 18 holes when he was 12; at 13 he broke 70. He perfected his golf game at Ohio State and won the United States Amateur Championship in 1959 and 1961 before turning professional. Nicklaus joined the professional tour at the time when the popularity of Arnold Palmer and expanded television coverage enhanced the game's popularity and purses. Jack gained widespread recognition when he defeated Palmer in a playoff to win the 1962 United States Open. Jack dominated golf for two decades and was at his top form in the most prestigious tournaments. From 1961 through 1977, Jack entered 63 major tournaments, winning 16, finishing second 13 times and third eight. The leader board seemed incomplete without Nicklaus' name.

Jack won the United States Open four times, and was runner-up four more times. He won the PGA on five occasions, the Masters six and the British Open three. He also has taken the Australian Open and the World Series of Golf four times and even won the British Amateur Championship. His tournament wins stretch across four decades from his United States Amateur victory in 1959 to the 1986 Masters. Nicklaus was the leading money winner more times than any other golfer, winning that crown in 1964, '65, '67, '71, '72, '73, '75 and '76.

Jack's concentration is his trademark. A deliberate player, he is at his best reading the subtle undulations of a green while blocking out the stares and noises of the tens of thousands who are watching him. No one thinks the game better than Jack, and when he hits the ball consistently the way he thinks, he cannot be beaten.

Many golfers drive farther than Nicklaus. For much of his career, his chip and pitch shots were ordinary. He putted well, especially the long ones. But Jack surpassed his rivals because he was probably the smartest golfer who has ever played the game. Jack's philosophy of the game is this: "Hitting the ball is really only half the game of golf. Once you become reasonably adept at that, how well you lay—how often you win or lose— depends almost entirely on how effectively you learn to manage the game's two ultimate adversaries, the course and yourself."

Perhaps the greatest compliment Jack ever received was from Bobby Jones, a person who knew something about dominating the game of golf. Bobby said, "Jack has a sound swing, constructed along classic lines, and majestic in its power, yet he is capable of a deftness in the strokes around the green that is astonishing in such a strong player ... Nicklaus plays a game with which I am not familiar."

Nicklaus is a success away from the golf course as well as on it. He and his wife have five children and his business empire is as far-flung as anyone's connected with sports. His specialty is designing golf courses and he has laid out some sticklers for his fellow professionals and other golfers to tackle.

But Jack is remembered by his fans as a fine gentleman, a wonderful sportsman. When Jack turned professional, he said that he hoped to be the greatest golfer the world has ever seen. Jack, you did it.

Jesse Owens established a world record for the long jump that lasted for more than a quarter of a century. (Courtesy Ohio State University Archives.)

James Cleveland Owens

"Jesse"
September 12, 1919–March 31, 1980

Jesse Owens was a great athlete, competitor, American, and person. He worked hard to be the best, and wore the champion's crown well.

Jesse, the son of an Alabama sharecropper and grandson of a slave, was born in 1919, just after World War I. His family moved to Cleveland when he was nine, and Jesse developed into a fine all-around athlete in Cleveland's playgrounds. A high school coach noticed his natural speed and helped Jesse develop into the finest high school trackman in the state of Ohio. An athletic scholarship to Ohio State was Jesse's ticket to stardom and away from the ghetto life.

Opposite: **Jesse Owens in 1935. (Photo courtesy Ohio State University Archives.)**

Jesse gave a hint of his potential when he set his first world record in the 1934 AAU Indoor Championships, with a long jump of 25 feet, 3¼ inches.

Jesse Owens became a national celebrity on May 25, 1935, when he broke five world records, and equalled a sixth, within a span of 45 minutes at the Big Ten track championships held at Ann Arbor, Michigan. At 3:15 PM Jesse opened with a 9.4 second 100-yard dash that equalled the existing world record. He then long jumped an incredible 26 feet, 8¼ inches, a world record that endured for nearly a quarter of a century. For encores, he won the 220-yard dash in world record time, eclipsing the 200-meter mark en route, and finished with a world record in the 220-yard low hurdles at 4:00, which also shattered the 200-meter low-hurdles world record.

Jesse had been suffering from a back injury after falling down a flight of stairs, and had to be helped into his coach's car to get to the track. When interviewed after his startling performance, Jesse summed up the difference between good and great athletic performance with his famous quote: "My back hurt when I went to the starting crouch, but when the starter said 'Get set,' I felt no pain at all."

Owens won four individual events, the 100- and 220-yard dashes, 220 hurdles, and the long jump, in meets ten times during the 1935 and 1936 seasons, and four other times won three individual events. Jesse won eight NCAA individual outdoors titles, the most ever recorded.

As good as he was, Jesse was not unbeatable at this stage of his career. In 1936, he lost three races to Eulace Peacock, and he failed to defeat Ralph Metcalf, the reigning "fastest human," until one week before the Olympics.

All track fans know that Owens won four gold medals at the 1936 Olympics, a feat finally equalled by Carl Lewis during the 1984 games, yet it is still difficult to imagine how good Jesse was that week of competition. Including trial heats, he competed 12 times and tied or broke the Olympic standard in nine of them. He beat Ralph Metcalf, later to become a United States Congressman, at 100 meters and Mack Robinson, Jackie's older brother, at 200 meters. After almost not qualifying in the preliminaries, he long jumped to an Olympic record of 26 feet, 5½ inches, a record that stood for 24 years until finally topped by Ralph Boston in 1960. Owens was not scheduled to run in the sprint relay, but was added to the team, along with another runner, as a last-minute replacement. Ironically, in an Olympiad tense with racial overtones brought on by host Adolf Hitler's "master race" beliefs, the two American runners who did not compete in the relay were Marty Glickman, later a noted sports announcer, and Fred Stolle, both of whom were Jewish. The American relay team, sparked by Owens, breezed to victory, and Jesse became a living legend.

Much has been written about Hitler's snubbing of Owens by leaving before Jesse was awarded his medals, but the matter has been exaggerated.

Actually, Hitler, perhaps disappointed with the competition's results, had taken to leaving the stadium early and had snubbed many others along with Owens. It was of little consequence. Jesse was too big a man to be bothered by what Adolf Hitler thought.

Through no fault of his own, Owens had a relatively short career. His last official competition was in August of 1936, in a dual United States–British Empire meet. Gathering war clouds ended most international competition for nearly a decade of what would have been his prime, and there were no professional events for Jesse to showcase his skills. Owens struggled financially, performing a few exhibitions such as racing thoroughbred horses, and when he got older, trotters, but he eventually did well as a public relations representative and goodwill ambassador. Jesse was a skilled public speaker and made as many as 200 personal appearances a year encouraging people to reach their full potential. He died of natural causes at Tucson, Arizona, in 1980.

Jesse competed on cinder tracks where conditions changed with the weather. Starting blocks were unknown in his day, nor were the training methods that turn out so many superb athletes today. Yet many of his records remained unbroken for decades. In 1950, Owens was voted the finest track athlete and the eighth best athlete overall of the first half of the 20th century by the Associated Press. Few will dispute his contribution to track and field in the United States.

Pele

Born: Edson Arantes de Nascimento
October 23, 1940–

Few athletes in the 20th century have dominated a sport as thoroughly as Pele has in soccer. From the time he joined the 1958 Brazilian national team until his retirement from the New York Cosmos of the North American Soccer League in 1977, Pele was regarded as the finest soccer player in this most international of sports.

Pele was born Edson Arantes de Nascimento in Tres Coracoes, Brazil, the son of Dondinho, a journeyman professional soccer player. Athletes in the back country of Brazil made little money in those days and Pele grew up in poverty. Soccer in Brazil, like boxing in the United States, provided an opportunity for fame and riches for poor youngsters. Pele wanted that chance.

Pele and his friends made a soccer ball from old rags tied with a string and played their games in the town's dusty lots. His playmates nicknamed him Pele when he was about eight years old, and although Pele claims he

Pele in 1977. (Courtesy of Milton Crossen Photo.)

has no idea of its significance, it probably came from the way he excelled in "peladas," the pickup soccer games played in vacant lots in Brazil's poor towns.

Pele found school difficult and uninteresting in a country where education is expensive and not mandatory. He dropped out of school in the fourth grade to play soccer as frequently as he could. He was so good at it that by the time he was fourteen, he was playing on the same team as his father, and at age fifteen he played for Santos, the finest team in Brazil and one of the finest in the world. Pele was considered the best soccer player in the world as a 17 year old, when he led Brazil to the World Cup in Stockholm in 1958.

Pele started slowly in the 1958 World Cup competition when an injured knee limited his game time during the opening rounds, but his goal, the only one scored in the game, won the quarterfinal match for Brazil over Venezuela. In the semifinals, Brazil topped France, 5–2, with Pele scoring three goals. Brazil won the championship, 5–2, over host Sweden with Pele scoring two goals and adding an assist. Pele returned to Brazil as its national hero, a niche he has yet to forfeit. Pele confirmed his reputation as the world's finest soccer player over the next four years playing for Santos. In 1962 he teamed with another brilliant player, Coutinho, and helped Brazil successfully defend the World Cup. Pele was continuously fouled in these games and missed several games through injury. Nationalism frequently replaces sportsmanship in World Cup competition, and skilled players like Pele can be victims of the strong-arm tactics of lesser-skilled players. The gentlemanly Pele simply said, "I will never play in World Cup competition again." His team had won two consecutive championships, so the best player in the world was not alibiing, but merely forcefully stating his feelings.

In 1966 England won the World Cup, and Brazil was eliminated early. Pele played, but his performance was again limited by injuries.

Pele was at his peak in the 1960s as his goal scoring became prodigious in a game known for low scoring. People from all over the world followed his progress when he approached the 1,000-goal plateau in 1969, a milestone comparable to hitting 700 home runs, or pitching 500 wins, in baseball. Previously, Jimmy McGrory of Scotland's Glasgow Celtics had become a soccer immortal by scoring 500 goals in an era in which defense was less emphasized. Goal 1,000 was scored on November 19, 1969, before 80,000 people at Rio Stadium and a nationwide Brazilian television audience, when Pele converted on a penalty kick. Pele was honored in virtually every arena in Brazil, and even journeyed to Alvorada Palace in Brasilia where Brazil's head of state presided over the official reception in his honor.

Twelve years after he had dominated World Cup play as a teenager, Pele came back to show the world what the "old man" could do. The scene was Mexico, 1970, and for the first time Pele completed the World Cup competition uninjured. Brazil won again, as it did for three of the four times Pele competed. Brazil swept through the early rounds with Pele scoring six goals in six games. He scored four in the three-game championship round, including the first goal in Brazil's 4–1 romp over Italy in the finale.

Pele always played striker, one of the forward positions, where he was expected to score, pass, control the ball with both feet, and drive teammates' passes past the opponent's goalkeeper with either his head or feet. He excelled at every aspect of the game. His 41-inch vertical leap would be the envy of most professional basketball players. He had natural speed, exceptional peripheral vision, and the endurance of a marathon runner. His two greatest characteristics, however, were his desire to win and his willingness to sublimate his personal goals for team productivity. He was the ultimate "team player."

Pele was the only soccer player to be on three World Cup championship teams, and was the youngest world champion ever (at age 17 in 1958). He was the top scorer in the São Paulo League for 10 consecutive years, 1957 through 1966, and added another scoring title in 1974. He is the only soccer player to score more than 1,000 goals in a career.

Pele retired from soccer in the early 1970s a rich man, the highest paid athlete of the '60s and '70s. But there was still one more world to conquer. The United States, the hotbed of sports throughout the entire century, knew little of soccer and cared less. Pele signed a contract with the New York Cosmos of the North American Soccer League in 1975 for $2 million per year for three years. Pele did not need the money, but could not resist the challenge of establishing soccer in the States. Pele single-handedly put soccer on the map in North America. He drew crowds of over 60,000 to games that would attract less than 10,000 if he were not playing. Although he was 34, an age considered "over the hill" in soccer, he scored 15 goals and had 14 assists in 23 games for the 1975 Cosmos. He led the Cosmos to the league championship in 1977. Pele played his last game on October 1, 1977, in Giants Stadium in the New Jersey Meadowlands for the New York Cosmos against his beloved Santos from Brazil. The game drew 77,691 fans, the largest attendance for a soccer game in the United States. When Pele retired, professional soccer in the United States rapidly declined. Within a few years, the North American Soccer League, built around Pele, ceased operations. But Pele's mission had not failed. Participants in youth soccer had numbered about 50,000 when Pele arrived in the States and now more than 600,000 young men and women take part.

These days Pele leads a quiet life with his wife and family in Brazil. He may be the one sports personality about whom an adverse word has yet to be spoken. He is still devoted to his family, soccer, and young people. He is still Pele, the poor kid from Brazil's outback who played soccer better than anyone else who ever lived.

Sugar Ray Robinson

Born: Walker Smith
May 3, 1921–April 12, 1989

Before he ever won a professional title, boxing fans called him "the uncrowned champ" and the greatest fighter, "pound-for-pound," then boxing. Many experts today regard "Sugar Ray" Robinson as the best fighter "pound-for-pound" who ever entered the ring.

"Sugar Ray" Robinson grew up Walker Smith in the Black Bottom section of Detroit, the same community that produced his idol, Joe Louis. His family moved to New York where he began boxing as an amateur. He won all of his 85 bouts en route to winning New York's Golden Gloves featherweight and lightweight titles. He trained at the Salem Crescent Club in Harlem with George Gainford, who later trained him professionally. It was Gainford who accidentally gave him his ring name, "Sugar Ray" Robinson. The story goes that young Walker Smith showed up for an amateur bout without the required AAU identification card. Gainford always carried a few spares, and handed Walker one saying "You're Ray Robinson tonight." A few months later, Gainford mentioned that young "Robinson" was the sweetest fighter in the club, and from then on, he was Sugar Ray Robinson.

Ray turned professional in 1940 and won his first 40 bouts, including wins over the past and future world champions Jake LaMotta, Fritzie Zivic, Sammy Angott and Marty Servo. His first loss came in February 1943, when Jake LaMotta out-pointed him in a close decision. After the loss to LaMotta, Robinson went undefeated for eight consecutive years, and by that time, he had avenged his loss to LaMotta four times.

Ray received his first title opportunity in December of 1946, when the welterweight championship was vacated. He easily defeated Tommy Bell, the second-leading contender, and became undisputed welterweight champion of the world in his 81st professional bout. Counting his amateur fights, Ray's career record at this point stood at 161–1. No welterweight was a match for him, and after 5 title defenses and numerous "over the weight" victories, Sugar Ray moved up from the 147-pound class to fight the 160-pound middleweights, where the purses were larger and good fighters more plentiful. He took the middleweight crown from old rival Jake LaMotta on February 14, 1951, by knocking him out in 13 rounds.

Sugar Ray then decided to take a Grand Tour of Europe and accepted a fight per week to cover expenses. He breezed through six opponents in six weeks, winning in Paris, Zurich, Liege, Antwerp, Berlin, and Turin. But the fight world was stunned, and Robinson embarrassed, when an out-of-condition Sugar Ray lost the middleweight title to England's Randy Turpin in a 15-round decision. Two months later in the Polo Grounds in New York, Turpin again gave Ray the fight of his life, opening a cut near Ray's right eye that threatened to end the fight at the end of the 9th round. With his back to the wall, Ray came out like a tiger in the 10th, and the lights went out for Turpin before the next bell sounded.

Robinson then went on to defend his title successfully against Carl "Bobo" Olsen and an over-the-hill Rocky Graziano, before moving up in weight again, this time for a big payday against Joey Maxim, the 175-pound champion.

Maxim could box, but was never much of a hitter. Robinson's toughest

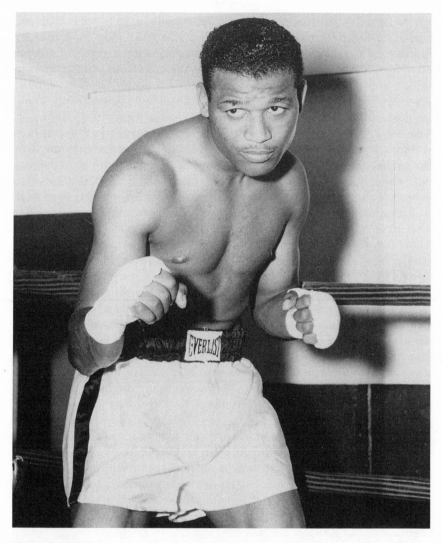

Robinson in 1955 prior to his bout with Ralph "Tiger" Jones. (Courtesy of AP/ Wide World Photos.)

opponent that night was the heat and humidity in New York's Madison Square Garden. Reports had the temperature at 104 degrees. Robinson easily outboxed Maxim and moved ahead in points. The referee suffered heat exhaustion after 10 rounds and was replaced. Robinson collapsed after 13, unable to answer the bell for round 14. The badly outclassed Maxim was declared the winner since he was the only one of the three original participants still standing when the bell rang for the 14th round.

Ray Robinson was always a showman in the ring and decided to retire for a career on the stage. He was an agile dancer with a great personality, and made as much as $15,000 per week when he started, but Astaire or Bolger he was not. Robinson returned to the ring after a two-year absence, at the age of 34, because he needed the money.

Robinson lost the second bout of his comeback to Ralph "Tiger" Jones, but on December 9, 1955, he defeated Bobo Olsen in two rounds to regain his middleweight title. Ray became a fighting champion, alternately losing and winning the middleweight title to some all-time greats, Gene Fullmer (twice), Carmen Basilio and Paul Pender. He lost the title permanently to the Fighting Mormon, Gene Fullmer, on a 15-round decision in 1961. His record at that time, against the best in the world, was 150–8.

It was time to quit, but Ray continued fighting until 1965, when he was 45. Like many great fighters he stayed on too long, losing in his last year to Memo Ayon, Stan Harrington (twice), Fred Hernandez, and Joey Archer. In his prime Sugar Ray could have taken them on, one after another, and have them all put away before the 10th round.

Ray devoted most of his post-ring career to the Sugar Ray Youth Foundation, a Los Angeles based program to help poor young people. He did some bit parts in movies and occasionally danced in an old pal's act in Las Vegas. But his stage performances never measured up to what he accomplished in the ring. There he always received rave notices.

George Herman Ruth

"Babe," "The Sultan of Swat"
February 6, 1895–August 16, 1948

For a period of more than 15 years, Babe Ruth was baseball. He was on the scene when the game's reputation was reeling from the Black Sox scandal (the attempt to fix the 1919 World Series). His personality and booming bat saved the game.

Much has been written of Roger Maris' feat of topping Babe's one season total of 60 home runs and Hank Aaron's surpassing Babe's career mark of 714 homers, but no one has approached Ruth's major league career.

Babe Ruth was born to a poor saloon keeper in Baltimore, Maryland, in 1895. Babe spent most of his first few years at his father's waterfront tavern learning the tough ways and colorful expressions of the seagoing customers. At age seven he was considered incorrigible and was shipped off to St. Mary's Industrial School where his parents hoped that the good Xaverian Brothers could instill some discipline in the tough, young kid and

The power in Ruth's awesome swing can be seen in this 1920 photo. (Courtesy of National Baseball Library, Cooperstown, N.Y.)

teach him a trade. He never became disciplined, nor did he make it as a tailor, the trade selected for him, but St. Mary's turned his life around. Babe met Brother Mathias at the school, and that 6-feet, 6-inch giant of a man immediately took a liking to Babe, taught him right from wrong, and introduced him to baseball. Young George was the school team's catcher, a lefthanded one at that, and pitched regularly. When he was 19, he signed

Opposite: **The Babe as a pitcher for the Boston Red Sox. (Courtesy of National Baseball Library, Cooperstown, N.Y.)**

a contract to pitch with the Baltimore Orioles of the International League and compiled a 22-9 record in his first year of organized baseball. The next year, 1914, he made his major league debut with the Boston Red Sox appearing in 14 games, winning two and losing one. From 1915 through 1919, he was one of the top pitchers in baseball, winning 87 while losing 45. His best year was 1916 when he was 23-12, with an earned run average of 1.75. The Red Sox won the pennant and World Series that year and Ruth beat the Brooklyn Dodgers 2–1 in 14 innings in the second series game, pitching a masterful six-hitter and shutting them out after the first inning. Boston finished second in 1917 despite Ruth's 24-13, 2.01 ERA season. Injuries held Ruth to 20 starts in 1918, but he was 13 and 7 during the regular season and the star of the World Series. Babe shut out the Cubs, 1–0, on six hits in the Series opener, and won the fourth game, 3–2, after completing a streak of 29⅔ scoreless World Series innings.

Ruth started playing the outfield when he was not pitching in 1918 and hit 11 home runs, enough to lead the American League in that dead ball era. In 1919, he hit an unthinkable 29, a major league record, while his closest competitor in the American League had 10 and the National League crown was won with 12. Limited to 15 starts, Babe had a creditable 9-5 season.

Babe Ruth was traded to the New York Yankees in 1920 in the greatest steal in sports history. Playing the outfield exclusively, Babe Ruth hit .376 and again set the all-time season home run record, this time with 54. The rest of the American League hit 215 home runs that year while the National Leaguers hit 261. Babe was just warming up for 1921, the best season any baseball player ever had.

Babe Ruth led the New York Yankees to their first pennant in 1921, when he upped the major-league home run record for a season to 59, batted .378, scored 177 runs, batted in 171, and walked 144 times. His slugging percentage, .846, was one point below his all-time high, set in 1920, and 81 points higher than any other ballplayer has ever achieved. In fact, Ruth's career slugging percentage of .690 is 56 points higher than runner-up Ted Williams' .634. Incidentally, he pitched twice in 1921 and had a 2-0 record.

Ruth waged a relentless assault on the record book. He led the American League in home runs 12 times, and had 11 seasons when he hit 40 or more home runs. Only ten major league players have hit 50 or more home runs in a season: five did it once, Mickey Mantle, Ralph Kiner, Jimmy Foxx and Willie Mays did it twice; Ruth four times. He scored more than 100 runs 12 times, leading the league in eight of those seasons, and twelve times he had more than 100 runs batted in.

People frequently associate Ruth with strikeouts, yet he never struck out more than 100 times in a season. He walked more than 100 times in 13 seasons, including 170 times in 1923. His 2056 career walks has been approached only by Ted Williams and is a safe bet to be the most in the century.

Despite his lifetime batting average of .342, and seasons hitting .376, .378, .393, .378, .372, and .373, he led the American League in batting only once.

Babe played in ten World Series with the Red Sox and the Yankees, had three Series wins with no losses, and an ERA of 0.87. He batted .326 in World Series play, had a slugging percentage of .744, hit 15 home runs, and even stole two bases in one inning. Babe Ruth made his final Series appearance in 1932 when the Yankees swept the Chicago Cubs. Ruth hit two homers in game three, including the one many spectators claim he "called," by pointing his bat toward the outfield fence before depositing the ball in the seats where he had pointed.

Babe was always a rowdy off the field and lived life to the fullest. His appetite for food, liquor, and women was reputed to be insatiable. He was popular with the press, loved to have his picture taken, and genuinely enjoyed the company of youngsters.

Babe was disappointed that he was never chosen manager of the New York Yankees. He spent his years after baseball in luxurious comfort, and never slowed his life style until throat cancer caught up with him in his final year. He died at the age of 53.

How good was Babe? He made the Hall of Fame as a batter, but if he had continued as a pitcher, he would have also qualified. He fielded well and was an intelligent base runner. He was the greatest sports drawing card of the 20th century.

They call Yankee Stadium "The House That Ruth Built." They could just as easily call baseball "the sport that Ruth saved."

James Francis Thorpe

"Jim," "Bright Path"
May 28, 1888–March 28, 1953

Jim Thorpe was the prototype of the modern athlete—big, strong, good speed, natural athletic skill, a winner, fearless, versatile, and for much of his career, virtually unbeatable. Thorpe set the standards at which the millions of 20th century athletes aim.

Jim Thorpe was born in Prague, Oklahoma, in 1886, a Sac and Fox Indian with a trace of Irish ancestry. He had limited schooling in his early years, and drifted from job to job as a cowboy and farmhand. The United States government ran a school for Native Americans in Carlisle, Pennsylvania, in those days, and Bright Path, as Jim was known to his friends on the reservation, was invited to attend. Jim Thorpe put the Carlisle Indian School into the history books.

Although Carlisle had an enrollment of only 500 students — and a 16-player football team — it competed with the best college teams. The game then was more brutal than it is now, with limited passing, virtually no equipment, few substitutes, and little finesse. Dozens of football-related deaths were recorded annually. Thorpe was fortunate to be coached at Carlisle by Pop Warner, the most innovative football mind of that era. Warner realized Thorpe's athletic potential, and in two years turned out a national power at Carlisle.

Jim Thorpe was an All-American in 1908 on a Carlisle team that defeated the University of Pennsylvania, Pittsburgh, Penn State, Nebraska, and Syracuse on its way to a 10-2-1 record. Thorpe was not a serious student and dropped out of school in 1909 to work as a farmhand in Pennsylvania; he also played semiprofessional baseball in North Carolina. Pop Warner convinced Jim to come back to school in 1911 by telling him that if he trained properly, he could earn a berth on the United States Olympic team in 1912.

The 1911 season was another All-American one for Thorpe, as he developed into the best all-around football player in the nation. He carried the ball, punted, drop kicked, passed, and received as well as anyone — and he played 60 minutes. He scored 15 points as Carlisle handed powerhouse Harvard its only loss of the season, 18–15.

Thorpe dazzled the Olympic selection committee at its tryouts in New York's Polo Grounds and they selected him to represent the United States in both the five-event pentathlon and the ten-event decathlon in the 1912 Olympics. Jim Thorpe's Olympic performance has yet to be surpassed. The pentathlon was conducted in one day, and Jim won the long jump, discus throw, 200-meter dash and 1,500-meter run. He finished third in the javelin throw. Decathlon competition extended over two days, and Thorpe won four of the 10 events — the high jump, shot put, 110-meter hurdles, and 1,500-meter run. He was third in the pole vault, long jump, discus and 100-meter dash and could only manage fourth in the 400-meter run and the javelin. He more than doubled the score of his nearest competitor, and set records that lasted for generations.

When he was presented his medals by King Gustav of Sweden, their brief dialogue perhaps summed up both the athletic ability and personality of Jim Thorpe.

"You, sir, are the greatest athlete in the world," said the monarch.

Thorpe replied, "Thanks, King."

It was back to Carlisle and football in the fall of 1912 and the Indians, led by Thorpe, had an outstanding season. Jim scored 22 points in a win over Army, setting the stage for the victory by returning the opening kickoff of the second half for an apparent touchdown. When it was called back because of a penalty, Thorpe took the ensuing kickoff and ran it back all

Jim Thorpe in 1951. (Courtesy of AP/Wide World Photos.)

the way again. He scored 198 points that season and had eight touchdown runs of 50 yards or more.

The following year the newspapers revealed that Thorpe had played baseball professionally for $60 per month. Jim readily admitted it because he had no idea that he was not permitted to play baseball for money and remain an amateur in other sports. In fact, unlike so many athletes who have taken money "under the table," Jim Thorpe never changed his name those two summers he played baseball in North Carolina. Jim returned his Olympic medals and they were redistributed to the runners-up.

Thorpe then began professional careers in both baseball and football. He was a fringe major league baseball player from 1913 until 1919, batting .252 in 201 games, mostly for the New York Giants. He never got along with

Giants manager John McGraw, and blamed him for his mediocre career. When he got away from McGraw, he hit .327 for the Boston Braves and once had seven consecutive pinch hits.

Professional football was haphazardly organized in Thorpe's day, and he starred for such teams as the New York Indians. He was player-coach for Canton in 1919, the first year the National Football League was formed, and the league even took advantage of his name to make him its first president in 1920. Thorpe was still playing football for the Chicago Cardinals in 1929 at the age of 41.

Jim Thorpe's later life had many sad days. He drank heavily, went through several marriages, and worked as a carnival worker and laborer. He died of lip cancer in March, 1953.

In 1950, the Associated Press voted Jim Thorpe the outstanding football player and all-around athlete of the first half of the 20th century. Although his Olympic medals were not returned to him during his lifetime, the International Olympic Committee reinstated his amateur status posthumously and recast his medals. It did not matter. Thorpe will always be remembered as one of the greatest athletes of all time.

John Unitas

"Johnny U"
May 7, 1933–

"You're too small, Johnny, you'll never make it at this level of football." John Unitas heard those words when he was in high school, college, and professional football. They must have come back to him when he was selected to the Football Hall of Fame in 1979, and more poignantly, when that body in 1972 chose him as the finest professional quarterback in the history of the game.

Things did not come easily for John Unitas. His father passed away when John was five, leaving his mother to raise a family of four. She drove a coal truck, worked in a bakery, scrubbed floors, and still found time to train herself to sell insurance and do bookkeeping. It is easy to see where John got his "never give up" attitude.

Unitas developed into a fine high school quarterback at Pittsburgh's St. Justin's High School, but was turned down for athletic scholarships by the powerhouse college football programs because his 6 feet, 145-pound frame seemed too fragile for big-time college football. But the University of Louisville, which ran a low-key program, offered Unitas a scholarship, and John gratefully accepted.

Unitas had a fine college career, even if he did not put Louisville on on the big-time football map. During Unitas' tenure at the college Louisville was 12-23, but Unitas completed 245 of 502 passes for 27 touchdowns, and was drafted in the ninth round by the Pittsburgh Steelers. Although he was now a muscular 190 pounds, Unitas was cut from the Steelers and spent the 1955 season playing sandlot football for the Bloomington Rams for six dollars per game.

. John Unitas did not look like a football player. His face was bony, his shoulders slumped, his toes pointed in, his legs were skinny, and his long, loose arms dangled at his side. But John was intelligent, and physically and mentally tough.

After signing with the Baltimore Colts as a free agent in 1956, John survived the cut, and rode the Baltimore bench as backup to their established quarterback, George Shaw. John got his opportunity during the fourth game of the season when Shaw broke his leg, and Unitas became a regular. John was a little erratic as he learned his trade, and Baltimore lost three games in a row as the season approached its finale against Washington. In that game, Unitas threw a 53-yard touchdown pass that led to a 19-17 victory that solidified his position as starting quarterback.

In 1957, the Colts added ends Raymond Berry and Jim Mutscheller to a team that already had Alan Ameche, Big Daddy Libscomb, Art Donovan, Lenny Moore, and L.G. Dupre. Within a year Baltimore became a contender, finishing second in the National Football League's Western Division, and Unitas was chosen as the league's Most Valuable Player. The following year the Colts were the terror of the NFL, and went all the way to the championship. The team won its first six games that year, but Unitas suffered fractured ribs and a punctured lung in the sixth game, a 56-0 rout of the Green Bay Packers. He was back three weeks later, however, his ribs protected by a special harness, and threw a 58-yard pass on the first play from scrimmage to lead the Colts to a 34-7 win over the Rams, and virtually insured the Western Division championship. The season culminated in Baltimore's 23-17 overtime victory over the New York Giants, a game generally considered to be the finest ever played.

John Unitas perfected the two-minute drill in that classic game. Trailing 17-14 with 90 seconds remaining, Baltimore took possession of the ball on its own 14-yard line, and Unitas went to work. John methodically moved his team down the field, completing four passes along the way. With nine seconds left, Unitas had the ball on the Giants' 20, and Steve Myrha kicked the field goal that sent the game into overtime. After an unsuccessful Giants' possession, Unitas, neatly mixing passes and running plays, engineered an 80-yard drive that resulted in an Alan Ameche touchdown from the one, and a Baltimore championship. Unitas was even better the following season, 1959, when he threw 32 touchdown passes to lead the Colts to the Western Division title again. Baltimore again defeated the

John Unitas publicity shot with the Baltimore Colts. (Courtesy of National Circuits Inc.)

Giants in the playoffs, this time 31–16. Unitas scored one touchdown and passed for two as he completed 18 for 29. That season Unitas won the Bert Bell Award as the league's outstanding player.

Consistency was Johnny's trademark, as his career statistics indicate. In 14 seasons, he completed 55 percent of his passes for over 35,000 yards, and 266 touchdowns. In the years between 1956 and 1960, he completed a touchdown pass in 47 consecutive games. With Unitas at the helm, the Colts were 185-63-4, won four Western Conference crowns, and three league championships. Unitas was selected for the Pro Bowl in 10 of his 16 professional seasons, and won the league's Most Valuable Player Award three times.

Unlike most quarterbacks of his era, Johnny called his own plays, even for such demanding coaches as Weeb Ewbank, Don Shula, and Don McCafferty. It is easy to see why. Unitas was one of the brightest, most reliable players in the history of football.

Theodore Samuel Williams

"The Splendid Splinter," "The Thumper"
August 30, 1918–

He stood at bat, tall, lean, patient, his full concentration focused on the pitcher. In came a fast ball that looked good to everyone in the stands. "Ball two!" barked the home plate umpire. The fans should have known. Ted Williams only swung at strikes.

Ted first broke into organized baseball as a 17-year-old, 6-3, 148-pounder when he signed with the San Diego Padres of the Pacific Coast League. Ted moved up to the majors with the Boston Red Sox in 1939, and the rookie immediately began abusing American League pitchers. He hit .327 that year with 31 home runs and 145 runs batted in — fine statistics for a left-handed hitter in Fenway Park (a right-handed hitter's paradise) but a demanding place for left-handed power hitters. For the next 18 years, Ted proved to be the finest hitter in modern baseball.

Ted grew up pretty much a loner in the San Diego area. He saw little of his parents, who divorced when he was young. His mother, an active Salvation Army worker, had little interest in sports, and was gone all day and half the night "working the streets for the Salvation Army," as Ted puts it. His dad ran a photography shop in downtown San Diego, and frequently did not get home until after ten o'clock. Ted taught himself to hit, and spent much of his time studying batting techniques and testing his theories in the San Diego playgrounds. He played a pickup game called "Big League," which required two players, a bat, and a ball. Williams always thought that the game featured the essence of baseball, the unending battle between pitcher and batter. Although Ted was a fine high school pitcher, he once said, "I would rather swing a bat than do anything else." Eddie Collins, the Hall of Famer and general manager of the Red Sox when Ted was in Boston, said that "Ted lived for his next at bat." His scientific approach to hitting has influenced batting coaches and many top hitters since.

Ted Williams in the 1950s. (Courtesy National Baseball Library, Cooperstown, N.Y.)

Ted's shyness and loner characteristics did not go over well with the Boston sportswriters who wrote many unfair things about him in the newspapers. Ted was accused of being a draft-dodger and not being nice to his mother, both untruths. His running feud with the press and the Boston fans became legend. Williams felt that many sportswriters were too interested in his personal, rather than his professional, life. Those who knew Ted found him personally charming, opinionated, stubborn, and a delightful companion.

Williams had several "best" seasons. In 1941, Ted was hitting .3999555 on the last day of the season, and since that rounded to .400, he could have sat out the final doubleheader and be the first player since Bill Terry, Ted's idol, to reach that goal. Instead, Ted played, went six for eight, and boosted his average to .406, a level that has not been matched since.

He and Rogers Hornsby are the only two people to win baseball's triple crown twice, leading the league in batting average, runs batted in, and home runs. In 1942, Williams' league-leading totals were .346, 36, and 141, and in 1947 his Triple Crown numbers were .343, 32, and 114. Ironically, because of his feud with the sportswriters, who select the league's Most Valuable Player, he was snubbed for the award in both seasons. Ted also had a standout year in 1957 when he led the American League with a .388 average as a 39-year-old, and followed that up with another batting championship one month past his 40th birthday.

Ted missed the 1943, 1944, and 1945 seasons serving as a fighter pilot during World War II in the Pacific. The stories about Ted's incredible vision started when the service doctors mentioned that he could see at 20 feet what most people could see at 10. Ted had the batting eye of any power hitter who ever played baseball, and earned his reputation for never swinging at bad balls. Ted claimed that he not only could see the bat make contact with the ball when he swung, but that he could see how many seams were on the part of the ball the bat struck.

Williams' career statistics, as awesome as they are, must be evaluated in light of the fact that he spent two hitches and five prime seasons in the military serice. He flew 38 combat missions over Korea as a Marine jet pilot. His lifetime batting average of .344 places him sixth on the all-time list, and first among the moderns. His lifetime slugging average, .634, is second only to Babe Ruth's. Ted hit 521 home runs, and would have gone over 700 if it were not for the service years. He led the league six times in runs scored, four times in runs batted in, eight times in walks, nine in slugging average and won six batting and four home run titles. Ted drove in more runs per at bat than anyone in the history of baseball except Babe Ruth, and got on base more times per at bat than anyone, including Ruth. He won the American League's Most Valuable Player Award twice, in 1946 and 1949, but probably should have won it four times. Ted was such a good hitter that in 1953, after serving close to two years in active combat, he rejoined the Red Sox lineup for the last 37 games of the season, and after minimal workouts, hit .407, with 13 home runs, and a slugging average of .901!

After retiring in 1960, Ted managed the Washington Senators for three years, winning Manager of the Year in 1969, but devoted much of his time to his second love, fishing. Elected to the Hall of Fame in 1966, the first year he was eligible, Ted was accorded an additional honor by the Hall in 1985, when he joined Babe Ruth as being the only two ball players to have life-sized wooden statues of them displayed in the museum. Ted is shown completing the powerful follow-through to his swing. Somehow you know that the pitch must have been over the plate.

The Runners-up

Muhammad Ali

Born: Cassius Marcellus Clay
January 18, 1942–

He came out of Louisville in 1960, the biggest fan of his own talents, proclaiming "I'm the greatest!" and spent the better part of the next two decades backing up that boast.

Cassius Clay, a slick young boxer with a questionable punch but blinding hand speed, won the Olympic light-heavyweight gold medal in Olympic boxing in 1960, and soon turned professional under the aegis of a group of Louisville businessmen. Clay had been an outstanding amateur boxer. He twice won National Golden Gloves titles and was a national AAU champion twice. His 6-3 frame filled out to 215 pounds, he added power to his punches, and began his march to the world's heavyweight championship.

Clay won all 19 fights, 15 by knockout, on his way to a championship bout, but was a 10 to 1 underdog when he faced Sonny Liston for the title in Miami Beach on February 25, 1964. In the first of two bizarre bouts with Liston, Clay, then 22 years old, won the title when Liston failed to answer the bell for round seven. Ironically, Cassius had almost failed to come out for the sixth round due to blurred vision, but trainer Angelo Dundee shoved him off the stool and into boxing's limelight. After winning the title, Clay announced his conversion to the Black Muslim religion, and changed his name to Muhammad Ali.

Ali kayoed Liston in the first round of their rematch at Lewiston, Maine, with a punch that few of the 2,344 spectators saw. He then successfully defended his heavyweight crown against former champion Floyd Patterson, George Chuvalo, Henry Cooper, Brian London, Karl Mildenberger, Cleveland Williams, Ernie Terrell, and Zora Folley.

Ali was stripped of the heavyweight title because of his anti-draft stand in 1967. After an enforced absence from the ring of several years he regained the title, first from George Foreman, knocking him out in the famous "Rumble in the Jungle." He defended the title ten more times before losing it in 1978 to 24-year-old Leon Spinks. Ali regained the title again by defeating Spinks in a rematch.

Muhammad Ali (Courtesy of Alan Dye).

Ali won two out of three bouts from each of his two toughest rivals, Joe Frazier and Ken Norton. In the classic series with Frazier, Smokin' Joe easily won the first bout in New York's Madison Square Garden, and Ali won the next two, the first by decision and the second, the famed "Thrilla in Manilla" by a knockout at the end of the 14th round. Norton, a tough former Marine, gave Ali three close battles. Norton broke Ali's jaw in the first round of their first bout and earned a close 12-round split decision. Ali won the next two meetings in tight, controversial decisions.

Like so many great fighters, Ali stayed on too long in the ring. At age 38 he was stopped by the fine heavyweight champion, Larry Holmes. When he lost a one-sided decision to Trever Berbick, even Ali knew the gloves must be hung up for good.

Ali dominated boxing for nearly 20 years. He won 56 of his 60 professional fights, 37 by knockout, and was decisioned four times. The son of a Louisville sign painter, the grandson of slaves, he became the most widely recognized face in the world. His skill and colorful style gave new life to boxing. He convinced more than one skeptic he was "the greatest."

Sammy Baugh

"Slingin' Sammy"
March 17, 1914–

Sammy Baugh was one of the most versatile players in the history of football. He earned his reputation mostly as a quarterback both in college and professionally, but he was also an outstanding defensive safety and one of the finest punters of all time.

Baugh was a blocking back in high school and was offered a baseball scholarship to the University of Texas. He opted for Texas Christian University, and instantly upgraded its football program. He first starred at TCU in 1935, a year the football had been made slimmer and easier to pass. Sammy was the first of the modern quarterbacks who realized that it was easier to move a team downfield by mixing passes with running plays, and not passing only in desperation. He threw the ball thirty or forty times per game when ten forward passes was considered normal for a college game. Texas Christian University went 11-1 in 1935, and was 8-2-2 in 1936, with Sammy at the helm. The Horned Frogs won both the Sugar and Cotton Bowls during Sam's tenure. In the 1936 Sugar Bowl against Louisiana State University, he punted 14 times on a muddy field, and averaged 48 yards per kick. He kicked several balls out-of-bounds inside the opponent's five-yard line, and also kicked a 55-yarder out of bounds from his own end zone.

Baugh's performances for Texas Christian made him a legend in the Southwest. A three-year All-American quarterback, he was chosen by the Football Writers Association as the All-Time, All-American college quarterback for the 50 years from 1919 until 1969. Yet Slingin' Sammy is better remembered as the star of the Washington Redskins from 1937 until 1952.

Ordinarily, football statistics of players from the 1930s, '40s and '50s, particularly passing statistics, do not hold up against those of today's players. Teams played only 10 or 12 games then, and football was a running game. The ball was rounder than today, and much harder to throw. Baugh did not even play from a T-formation for his first six years in the pros; the Redskins used a double wing until 1944. But Sammy Baugh was the National Football League's leading passer in 1937, '40, '43, '47, and '49. Sammy led Washington to five Eastern Division titles and the National Football League Championship in 1937 and 1942. His best season was 1949 when he threw for 2938 yards and 25 touchdowns. He completed 56.5 percent of his passes in a 16-year NFL career, and over 70 percent in 1945, in an era when teams did not use flankers and wide receivers, today's receiving specialists. When Sammy retired from the National Football League he held the league record for most passes attempted, most completions, most touchdown passes, most yardage passing, and highest percentage of completions both in a season and a career.

Baugh never lacked confidence. One time, Washington Redskin coach Ray Flaherty, in diagramming a play for Baugh, showed him where the intended pass receiver would be and instructed Sam, "Hit him in the eye!" Sam smiled and said, "Which eye?"

Baugh had many great days in professional football. In 1948, he threw for 446 yards against Boston, the most passing yardage in a game up to that point. In 1947 against the Chicago Cardinals, he threw six touchdown passes while connecting on 25 passes for 355 yards.

Sammy may have been football's finest all-time punter with a career average of 44.9 yards, and a season's best average of 50.4 yards on 35 punts in 1940. Sam has recorded punts of 74, 75, 76, 81, and 85 yards in NFL play. Sam was a two-way player who excelled on defense and made 28 career interceptions playing safety. He was so versatile, that in 1943 he led the NFL in passing, punting, and interceptions.

Sammy's clutch performance won the 1937 NFL championship game against the Chicago Bears when he completed 18 of 33 passes for 335 yards including touchdown passes of 35, 55, and 75 yards on a frozen, torn-up field. He also made a game-saving tackle in the last minute of play to complete a Most Valuable Player performance.

After retiring as an active player, Baugh coached Hardin-Simmons, and later, the New York Titans. He retired from sports during the 1960s to manage his 35,000-acre cattle farm.

Baugh is a member of both the college and professional football Halls of Fame. He was selected to the NFL's 11-man All-Pro Team in 1937, 1940, and 1948 (there were no teams selected from 1943 to 1945), and was picked by the Hall of Fame selection committee for the All-Pro squad of the 1940s. On the occasion of the 50th anniversary of the NFL, the Professional Hall of Fame selectors chose Sam as runner-up to John Unitas as the All-Time NFL quarterback.

Robert Joseph Cousy

"Cooz," "The Houdini of the Hardwood"
Aug. 9, 1928–

When Bob Cousy completed his college career at Holy Cross and was eligible to play professional basketball, it seemed like no team really wanted him. His college record was impressive. He was a *Sporting News* All-American in 1950 and a second-string selection in 1949. He played on the 1947 Holy Cross team that won the NCAA championship. In college, he averaged 15.2 points, 7.5 assists, and 5.1 rebounds per game in his four-year stint. But the cognoscenti thought that his slim 6' 1" frame was too fragile, and his passes too fancy, for the "big boys" who played in the pros. Cousy proved them wrong.

Bob Cousy was a 1950 first round draft choice of the Tri-Cities franchise of the National Basketball League, but was traded immediately to the Chicago Stags. When the Stags folded that summer, the names of the Chicago players were put into a hat and drawn by the existing teams. Boston's coach, Red Auerbach, was disappointed when his team did not draw Andy Phillip's nor Max Zaslofsky's name, and he was stuck with Cousy. Red's disappointment was short-lived.

Bob Cousy quickly became professional basketball's second superstar, joining George Mikan at that plateau. Cousy passed and dribbled like no one before him and few since. He was the first player to pass behind his back regularly, and in those days before the 24-second clock, Cousy became famous for running out the clock by dribbling the ball. He was so good at it, that in one game against the New York Knickerbockers in 1960, Cousy dribbled the ball for the last 23 seconds of the game with no Knickerbockers getting close enough to him to commit a foul.

Bob could do just about anything on a basketball court, but he excelled as a playmaker and leader. His legendary peripheral vision and teamplay attitude enabled him to lead the league in assists for eight consecutive years from 1953 through 1960. And Cousy would score, as his 18.5 points per game average will attest. He once scored 50 points in a playoff game, the first time that feat had been accomplished.

Cousy developed the reputation of wanting the ball when the game was on the line. In one 1954 game against the Knickerbockers, Cousy came alive with 30 seconds remaining and the Celtics trailing by four points. Bob stole the ball twice and scored both times to force an overtime period. The Celtics finally won the game in double overtime with Cousy scoring 12 of the 20 points in the extra sessions. Performances like these were just another day at the office for Bob Cousy.

Cousy was a first-string NBA all-star from 1952 until 1961, and a second-string star in 1962 and 1963. He reached his full potential in 1956 when Bill Russell joined the Celtics to sweep the defensive boards and begin the fast break that Cousy engineered as well as anyone. Cousy was the league's Most Valuable Player that season, the second year in which the award was given. The Cousy-Russell Celtics won the NBA championship six of the seven years they were teammates.

Bob Cousy, like so many basketball stars, was a product of the New York City playgrounds. His parents were French immigrants who settled near Idlewild (now Kennedy) Airport in Queens. Bob graduated from Andrew Jackson High School in 1946 before emigrating to New England.

Above: **Bob Cousy makes the "impossible" pass to an open Celtic teammate. (Courtesy of Naismith Memorial Basketball Hall of Fame, Springfield, Mass.)** *Opposite:* **Sammy Baugh passing in his college days at TCU. Notice the old-fashioned helmet and the shape of the football. (Courtesy of Texas Christian University.)**

After retiring as a player, Bob coached at Boston College for three seasons, and in the NBA for four more. Since then, he has filled a variety of positions including a 5-year stint as commissioner of the North American Soccer League.

Bob Cousy was the finest player of his day. He revolutionized the game of basketball, perfected the fast break, and was instrumental in beginning the great dynasty known as the Boston Celtics. He truly was the "Houdini of the Hardwood."

William Harrison Dempsey
"Jack," "The Manassa Mauler"
June 24, 1895–May 31, 1983

Jack Dempsey's boxing style of boring straight in while constantly throwing punches made him one of the most popular athletes of all time. The style caused him to be knocked down several times, but the rugged battler always got up swinging until he connected with either of his dynamite-laden fists.

Jack was born in Manassa, Colorado, a mining town that blossomed and died in the 1890s. Jack was one of eleven children raised by poor sharecroppers in Colorado, and later in Utah. He left school at 15 to work in the silver mines but soon took to riding the rails as a hobo and earning meal money by challenging anyone in the tough frontier saloons who would fight him in a winner-takes-all match.

He worked his way west to San Francisco where he teamed up with Jack "Doc" Kearns, one of the great showman of that era. The two began a well-planned campaign to win the heavyweight boxing title. In his first four years in the ring, Dempsey recorded 26 first round knockouts, still the highest total in the record books. In 1918, when he was 23 years old, he won 21 of 21 fights, 17 by knockout. He kayoed contender Fred Fulton in 18 seconds and nailed Carl Morris, who had previously fought for the title, in 14 seconds. The stage was set for a title bout with Jess Willard, a non-fighting champion who had won the title from Jack Johnson in 1915 in 26 rounds and had not defended it since. On July 4, 1919, Jack Dempsey won the heavyweight championship from Jess Willard in four rounds in Toledo, Ohio. Willard, an awkward, slow-moving giant at 6′ 3″, 245 pounds, was a sitting duck for Dempsey who, although only 6 feet tall and a little over 180 pounds, floored him seven times in the first round. Jack won the title when Willard was unable to answer the bell for the fourth round. Jack Dempsey and Doc Kearns made boxing a big-time sport.

Jack successfully defended the title six times in the seven years he held it from 1919 until 1926, and each defense was a major sporting event. One

William Harrison Dempsey (Courtesy of Wide World Photos).

of Jack's defenses was a fourth-round knockout of French light-heavyweight champion Georges Carpentier in boxing's first million-dollar gate. Dempsey then took two years off until a worthy challenger who could fill a stadium emerged. In 1923, Dempsey out-pointed Tom Gibbons in 15 rounds as he prepared for one of the most sensational bouts ever recorded, against Luis Angel Firpo, the "Wild Bull of the Pampas," from Argentina.

As round one began, Dempsey missed a right and Firpo landed a crusher, downing the champion. Dempsey fought in a fog after that, but with the fierceness of a wounded tiger. Dempsey later said, "I was trying to keep from being killed." Before the round was over, Firpo had been down seven times and Dempsey had been sent through the ropes by Firpo's "half shove, half punch" right hand. Eyewitnesses differ on how long Dempsey was out of the ring, maybe it was seven or eight seconds, maybe it was eleven or twelve, but he returned half shoved, half scrambling, to floor his powerful opponent. The bell ended the round with both men exhausted. Dempsey won in 57 seconds of the second round after flooring Firpo three more times. Grantland Rice, the most famous sportswriter of that era, claimed that the Dempsey-Firpo fight was his greatest thrill in sports.

Dempsey met his match in 1926, after a three-year layoff, when boxing-master Gene Tunney cleanly beat him on a 10-round decision. Dempsey looked rusty and was a shadow of his former self. The rematch at Chicago's Soldiers Field on September 22, 1927, again won by Tunney, contained the famous long count. Tunney was floored for 17 seconds in the 7th round with the long count delayed because Dempsey hesitated before going to a neutral corner. No one knows for sure whether or not Tunney could have beaten the count if it were not for the mix-up.

Dempsey was through with big-time boxing after the Tunney matches, although he fought as many as 56 more bouts and exhibitions. Although his formal education was limited, Jack was self-educated and became one of the more beloved of the sports personalities. He was noted for his friendly greeting and his generosity. He served as a commander with the Coast Guard during World War II and became a successful restaurateur and a familiar face among fight fans near New York's Times Square. Dempsey died of natural causes at the age of 87.

Henry Louis Gehrig

"The Iron Horse"
June 19, 1903–June 2, 1941

Lou Gehrig was a large, rugged man of few words who allowed his performances to speak for themselves. Although overshadowed by his more flamboyant teammate, Babe Ruth, most of his career, Lou is without a doubt one of the finest baseball players of all time.

Lou Gehrig was born into poverty on New York City's upper east side. His father was a handyman and his mother a cook for the Sigma Nu fraternity of Columbia University. He attended New York High School of Commerce where he was an ordinary baseball player on a championship high school team. He achieved some degree of acclaim, however, when as a 15-year-old in an intercity championship game against Chicago's Lane Tech, he hit one over the right-field fence at Wrigley Field. Friends at Columbia helped Lou earn a football scholarship to the school, where Gehrig played tackle and fullback on the football team, and starred in baseball. When Lou's mother required an operation, Lou dropped out of school and signed with the New York Yankees to pay for it. In one of life's ironies, Lou's mother, who was frequently ill and required many operations, outlived her robust son.

Lou Gehrig was a winner. He batted cleanup for the great Yankee teams of the 1920s and 1930s. The Yankees finished seventh in 1925, Lou's rookie year, but during the remainder of his career, the Yankees won seven pennants, finished second in the American League five times, and third only once. Lou's Yankee teams won six of the seven World Series in which he played, winning 27 games while losing only 7.

Lou Gehrig was peerless in World Series play. In seven World Series he hit ten home runs, batted .361, and drove in 35 runs in 34 games. He dominated the 1932 Series in which the Yankees swept the Chicago Cubs. In the first game he hit a two-run homer and scored three times. In game two, he had three hits and followed that up with two homers in the third game, and three runs batted in and two runs scored in the fourth and last game. Gehrig was selected as the World Series Most Valuable Player four times during his career.

Gehrig could hit for both power and average, as his 493 career home runs and .340 lifetime batting average attest. He hit over 40 home runs in five seasons and led the league in homers three times. His .363 batting average won the batting crown in 1934. Lou averaged only 56 strikeouts per season while collecting an average of 107 bases on balls.

Despite these remarkable numbers, baseball fans best remember Lou Gehrig for his run production, durability, and leadership. Lou drove in over 100 runs in every season from 1926 through 1938, leading the league five times with totals of 175, 142, 174, 184 and 165.

Lou hit 23 career grand slams, a mark never since approached in baseball history. On June 3, 1932, he became the first player to hit four consecutive home runs in one ball game and was actually robbed of a fifth by Al Simmons' spectacular catch.

Lou earned his reputation as the "Iron Man" by appearing in 2130 consecutive games, one of the greatest sports feats of the 20th century, and almost double anyone else's string. He accomplished this with a tremendous display of courage. Late in his career, x-rays of his hands showed 17 fractures which Lou ignored as he continued to play.

When Gehrig broke into the major leagues, he was awkward and considered a liability in the field. By the end of his career, he played first base with the best of them. He once said, "In the beginning, I used to make one terrible play a game. Then I got so I'd make one a week, and finally, I'd pull one about once a month. Now I'm trying to keep it down to one a season." What Lou accomplished, he did with hard work.

During the 1938 season, Lou's health began to fail. People noticed that he frequently dropped things and that his hands shook. Still, he hit .295 and played every game. The following season, Lou played the first eight games and was hitting .143 when he went to Yankee manager Joe McCarthy and asked to be removed from the lineup, never to return. Lou's last appearance at the Stadium was on July 4, 1939, at Lou Gehrig Day when he spoke these now immortal words, "...today, I count myself the luckiest man on the face of the earth." There was not a dry eye in the house.

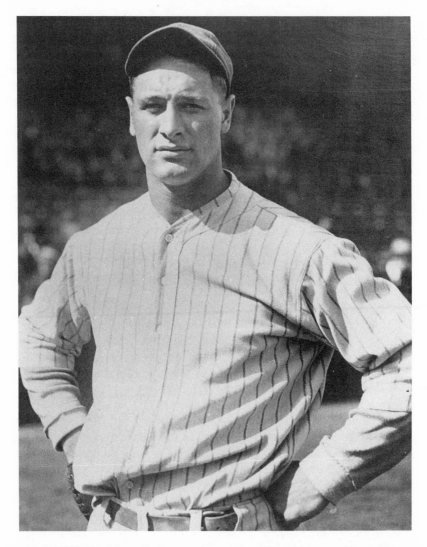

Lou Gehrig in his prime, during the late 1920s. (Courtesy of National Baseball Library, Cooperstown, N.Y.)

Lou's athletic ability and personal character were captured by Gary Cooper's portrayal of him in the classic movie, *Pride of the Yankees*. He was the finest baseball player of the 1930s and he left a legacy of leadership, sportsmanship, and class for players and fans to remember. He died in 1941, at the age of 37, from amyotrophic lateral sclerosis, now called Lou Gehrig's disease, a little more than two years after his incredible endurance streak was snapped.

Red Grange on his way to a touchdown against Michigan in 1924, in the game in which he turned in the finest performance in the history of college football. (Courtesy of University of Illinois.)

Harold Edward Grange

"Red," "The Galloping Ghost"
June 13, 1903–

Red Grange was 50 years ahead of his time as a football player. He was an open-field runner in the style of Gayle Sayers and Walter Payton, when football was best described as "three yards and a cloud of dust." He did more to popularize and revolutionize football than anyone in the 20th century.

Red Grange was a midwesterner from Wheaton, Illinois, who led the "Fighting Illini" of Illinois University to football prominence. He debuted for Illinois in a 1923 game against Nebraska, scoring three touchdowns in a 24–7 win. Illinois finished with an 8–0 record that year and Grange earned All-American honors, although he was just beginning to get the hang of how to run with the football.

Red Grange and famous jersey after his last Illinois game. (Courtesy of University of Illinois.)

Grange captured the imagination of sports fans everywhere on October 18, 1924, in the first game played at Illinois' new stadium at Champaign. The opponent was archrival Michigan, undefeated since 1921, and Grange put on the finest exhibition of running that football has ever seen. Red ran through the Wolverines like they were high school players who got off the bus at the wrong stadium. When they tried to tackle him, Grange slipped through their arms like a "Galloping Ghost." Red scored a touchdown the first four times he carried the football with runs of 95, 67, 56, and 44 yards, all within the first 12 minutes of play. At that point, his coach, Bill Zuppke, sat him down until half-time. In the third quarter, Grange ran for another touchdown and passed for a sixth in the final quarter. Grange rushed for 402 yards on 21 carries, and had six pass completions. No player in major college or professional competition has approached this feat.

The romp against Michigan was typical of what Grange could do. In 1925, he single-handedly derailed the University of Pennsylvania from its track to the national title by scoring runs of 60 and 55 yards. Red repeated as an All-American in both 1924 and 1925. He scored 31 touchdowns and ran for 3,637 yards in his three-year college career. Red's orange and blue number 77 jersey was retired when he graduated, just as his number was retired by the Chicago Bears at the end of his professional career.

Professional football was struggling in the early 1920s. "Papa Bear" Halas coached and played for a franchise that represented several midwestern towns before becoming the Chicago Bears. The big gate attraction was Jim Thorpe, an aging war horse, ten years past his prime. Grange was the foundation upon which the National Football League was established.

The disorganized and unrecognized world that was the NFL in those days gained credibility when Grange turned professional. He played during the regular season and barnstormed in the off season, filling stadiums wherever he went. Grange and the Chicago Bears played an 18-game postseason schedule in 1925, as they travelled from coast-to-coast popularizing professional football. Red packed them in. A record gate of 70,000 showed up at New York's Polo Grounds to see him play. Grange reportedly received $25,000 of the $100,000 gate that day and returned an interception for a touchdown. He received an unheard of $30,500 to play his first professional game for the Bears, and was so important to their appeal that when he could not play one game in Detroit, over $18,000 in receipts had to be returned to the fans.

The Red Grange/Chicago Bear tour (Red got top billing) probably netted Red a quarter of a million dollars, an incomprehensible amount during the 1920s.

Red made a movie in 1926, *One Minute to Play,* that met with both popular and critical acclaim. He followed that up with *Racing Romeo* and *The Galloping Ghost,* and even had a candy bar and a doll named for him. Red was the first player to hire an agent, the famous Cash and Carry Pyle, who made Grange a highly marketable commodity.

A rival American football league was established around Grange in 1926, and he starred for the New York Yankees. The league folded in one year, and the Yankees were absorbed into the National Football League with Grange as its star. Red missed most of the 1928 season because of a knee injury, and played with the Chicago Bears from 1929 through 1934. The knee injury deprived Red of much of his speed, yet he still excelled as a defensive player. He was good enough, however, to make the NFL's first

11-man All-Pro team in 1931. His coach, George Halas, said of his performance at that part of his career, "He was the game's greatest runner until he hurt his knee and after that, the game's greatest defensive back."

The Football Writers Association selected Grange as the All-American College Back for the 50-year era from 1919 until 1959, and the Professional Football Hall of Fame chose him as one of its original enrollees when the Canton shrine opened in 1963.

Football owes much to Red Grange, the person who made the game fun to watch.

Eric Arthur Heiden

June 14, 1958–

Eric Heiden is generally considered to be the finest speed-skating competitor of all time. Ironically, he comes from a country in which speed-skating meets are rarely held, and finding a rink is virtually impossible.

Eric was born in Madison, Wisconsin, to sports-minded parents. His father was an orthopedic surgeon who specialized in sports medicine; his mother, a locally well-known tennis player and swimmer. Eric's grandfather was the first person to interest him and his sister, Beth, in skating when he took them regularly to the local ponds. Eric and Beth eventually joined a speed-skating club in Madison, where they both developed into world-class competitors. Eric was spotted there by Diane Holum, a student at the University of Wisconsin and an Olympic gold medalist in speed skating. She set up a training program for the Heidens to develop their potential for international competition. Soon the training paid off.

Eric Heiden was not quite ready for the 1976 Winter Olympics held at Innsbruck, Austria — he finished seventh and nineteenth in the two events he entered. Several weeks later, he placed fifth in the overall world championship. From then on, the 19-year-old was unbeatable.

Heiden began in the 1977 campaign by winning the men's world speed-skating championship at Heerenveen, in the Netherlands, where he set a world record in the 500-meter event. Within the next two weeks, he won both the world junior all-around title and the world sprint championship. He repeated all three victories in 1978, and set world records at 1,000 and 3,000 meters. In 1979, he swept all the major titles, adding the 10,000-meter world record to his collection. Although he was virtually unknown in the United States, Heiden was an idol in Europe. In Norway, the recording "The Ballad of Eric Heiden" was a smash hit.

Eric Heiden gave the finest exhibition of speed skating, and one of the finest sports performances of all time, when he won all five speed-skating

Eric Heiden (on right) at the 1980 Winter Olympics.

events at the 1980 Winter Olympics at Lake Placid. On February 15 he won the 500-meter sprint. The next day, he set a new Olympic record winning the 5,000-meter race, and on the 19th, he added the 1,000-meter title, also establishing a new Olympic record. On February 21 he set still another Olympic record, winning at 1,500 meters. On February 23, Eric pulled out all the stops to win his fifth gold medal, this time setting an Olympic and world record at 10,000 meters.

Unlike many successful Olympic athletes, Eric shunned the limelight and had no interest in exploring commercial opportunities. He competed regularly in cycling, where his 29-inch thighs made him an instant contender in road racing, but Eric never trained seriously for the sport, and was a steady, but unspectacular, performer. He returned to his studies, graduating from Stanford University with a degree in science as he prepared for a medical career. Eric has been frequently seen since his Olympic success as a television commentator covering both cycling and skating events.

Sonja Henie
"The Pavlova of the Ice"
April 8, 1912 — October 12, 1969

One of the finest athletes of the 20th century was a petite 5′ 2″, 105-pound bundle of energy, Sonja Henie. Her success as a movie star sometimes overshadows her accomplishments as an athlete. Sonja's sophisticated style revolutionized figure skating, and her dynamic personality established the sport's popularity both in Europe and America.

Henie was born in Oslo, Norway, on April 8, 1912. Both her parents had inherited fortunes and her father operated the largest furrier business in Europe. Sonja's father was a world-class athlete, having twice won the world's cycling championship, and was one of Norway's best in speed skating, ski jumping and cross country skiing. Sonja's first love, however, was dancing, and she began ballet lessons when she was two. She won her first skating competition in speed skating at five, and by the time she was eight was unbeatable in age-group figure skating. Her execution, influenced by her ballet background, was decidedly different from the stiff movement considered good form in her early days. As a 10-year-old, she was 50 years ahead of her time in figure-skating style.

Henie won the Norwegian women's figure skating title in 1923, just after her 10th birthday, and qualified for the first Winter Olympics in Charmonix, France, in early 1924. She finished 8th and last, but after that, she would never again be defeated in an ice skating championship. She won the world's figure-skating championship in 1927 as a 13-year old, her first of 10 consecutive world titles. She was the world champion from 1927 until 1936, the year she turned professional. Sonja was known universally as the "Pavlova of the Ice."

Henie was equally unbeatable in Olympic competition, winning in 1928 at St. Moritz, 1932 at Lake Placid, and 1936 at Garmisch-Partenkirchen, each time by large margins. She won the Norwegian national championship each of the ten years in which she entered. With no competition in sight, she turned professional after the 1936 Olympics and toured

Courtesy of World Figure Skating Museum, Colorado Springs, Co.

in her own ice show, but her driving ambition was to be a movie star. Henie once said, "I want to do with skates what Fred Astaire is doing with dancing. No one has ever done it in the movies, and I want to."

Sonja Henie's record in major competition from 1923, when she was 11, until 1936, when she turned professional at the age of 34, is shown below. The blanks represent events which were either not held, or in which she did not compete.

Year	*Championship*
1923	Norwegian
1924	Norwegian
1925	Norwegian

Year		*Championship*		
1926	Norwegian	World		
1927	Norwegian	World		
1928	Norwegian	World	European	Olympic
1929	Norwegian	World	European	
1930		World	European	
1931		World	European	
1932		World	European	Olympic
1933		World	European	
1934		World	European	
1935		World	European	
1936		World	European	Olympic

In addition to her skating abilities, Henie was Norway's third-ranked woman tennis player and was an outstanding swimmer, equestrienne, and ballet dancer.

Sonja Henie became America's sweetheart in the late 1930s, and by the early 1940s was one of Hollywood's top box-office draws. She made over $50,000,000 during her skating and movie career. She lived the life of a movie queen, collecting jewelry and furs, was married three times and had many publicized romances, the most famous with Tyrone Power. Leukemia claimed her on October 12, 1969. For all practical purposes, Sonja Henie invented the sport of ice skating as it is known today. Her consistency in competition, and the margin by which she dominated her contemporaries, has not been approached by any other figure skater in this century.

Rogers Hornsby

"Rajah"
April 27, 1896–January 5, 1963

Rogers Hornsby broke into the major leagues as a "good glove, no hit," scrawny 140-pound shortstop who had batted .232 and .277 in his two minor league seasons. His hitting improved in his first five years with the St. Louis Cardinals where he averaged .309, and he developed into a decent-fielding shortstop. In 1920, his sixth with the Cardinals, he made several adjustments and became one of baseball's all-time superstars.

Hornsby spent the off season before the 1920 season doing heavy farm work and building a muscular, 180-pound body. In spring training, he also moved to second base and immediately became the best in baseball at that position. He led the National League in batting the next six seasons consecutively, hitting .370, .397, .401, .384, .424, and .403. Between 1921 and 1926 he averaged .402, and his .424 batting average in 1922 is the highest season average ever recorded in the majors.

(Courtesy of National Baseball Library, Cooperstown, N.Y.)

Make no mistake, Rogers Hornsby was no slap hitter. In the three years he hit over .400, he averaged 35 home runs per season and led the league twice in home runs. Rogers hit 42 homers in 1922, and 39 in 1925, and won the league's Triple Crown for leadership in batting average, home runs, and runs batted in both seasons. Only Ted Williams has won the Triple Crown twice since. Hornsby is second in career batting average, and seventh in career slugging average, numbers no right-handed batter approaches.

Hornsby continued batting at close to that pace until 1930, when he sustained a severe leg injury that diminished his skills. He should have quit then, but he continued for seven more seasons with subpar performances.

Rogers (it was his mother's maiden name) was second to Ty Cobb in two respects: his lifetime batting average, .358, is below Cobb's .367, and only Cobb, among the all-time greats, was harder to get along with. Rogers' stubbornness led to his being traded five times during his playing career, and in the eleven years he managed in the majors, he seldom got along with management, the press, or his players. He coached with the New York Mets in 1962, his last year in baseball, and wrote a book that season, called *My War with Baseball,* that summed up his off-field activities. Rogers was brutally frank, cold, aloof and independent. He said exactly what was on his mind. Once, when asked if there were any pitchers he feared, he said, "No, I feel sorry for them."

Rogers was an almost exact contemporary of Babe Ruth, yet the two stars contrasted in almost every respect. Ruth played in New York in the American League, was outgoing, loved people, especially children, and his eyes twinkled mischievously. Ruth attempted to drain from life's cup as much enjoyment as he could in the half century that was allotted him. Rogers was an introvert, played in the National League, in St. Louis, was sarcastic, and as Billy Herman, his great teammate, once said, "He would stare at you with those cold eyes." As for enjoying life, Rogers admitted, "Baseball is my life, the only thing I know and can talk about, my only interest." In his prime, Hornsby would not go to a movie or read a book, because he was afraid it might affect his batting eye.

Hornsby's sole vice was that he played the horses too frequently, yet he owned 15 percent of the St. Louis Cardinals by 1926. No one liked him. Babe had virtually every vice, and went through money as quickly as he earned it. Babe was the most popular athlete in the 20th century. Clyde Sukeforth, a veteran major-league player and manager, summed up the consensus evaluation of Hornsby's skills when he said, "When he had a bat in his hands, he had nothing but admirers."

His playing skills are unquestioned. He was one of the few truly great ball players who could hit for average, hit for distance, run, throw, and catch. He is generally considered the greatest second baseman of the 20th century.

Walter Perry Johnson

"The Big Train"
November 6, 1887–December 10, 1946

The strong, raw-boned, 19-year-old rookie had only one pitch, a fast ball, but it was the fastest that any batter, before or since, has seen. The scouting report on Walter Johnson that made the Washington Senators take notice was simply, "He knows where he's throwing, because if he didn't, there would be dead bodies all over Idaho." When he signed with the Senators in 1907, they had finished no higher than sixth in the eight team American League since its first year, 1901. It took three years for young Walter Johnson to master his trade, but from 1910 through 1919, he won 20 games every season even when playing for mediocre and poor teams, five of which had losing records.

Walter threw his blazer side-armed after an almost casual wind-up. His speed simply overpowered right-handed batters, and although the lefties got a better look at the ball, they too had little success against Johnson. One opposing batter summed up Johnson's speed when he said, "You can't hit what you can't see." Fortunately for American League hitters, Johnson was deathly afraid of hurting a batter with a pitch, and never deliberately threw at one.

Walter Johnson won 416 games, the most by a pitcher in the 20th century. His winning percentage of .599 was compiled with Washington Senator teams that played .489 ball. His lifetime earned run average of 2.17 over 21 seasons indicates how good he was. Johnson completed 532 of the 666 games he started, pitched 5,925 innings, and had 3,499 strikeouts.

Walter's finest season was 1913, when he won 36 and lost 7, compiling a 1.09 earned run average. He had 12 shutouts that year, threw five one-hitters, had 56 consecutive scoreless innings (an American League record that still stands), struck out 243 batters, and walked only 38. The Senators finished second with a 90-64 record, but were 6½ games behind the Philadelphia Athletics. Johnson's teammate, rookie Joe Boehling, was a decent 17-7, but the rest of the Senator staff was 37-50.

Johnson was 36 years old before he made his first World Series appearance in 1924 when the Senators defeated the New York Giants in seven games. He earned the starting assignment in the first game by winning 23 games during the regular season, and leading the American League in strikeouts.

Walter lost the first game, 4-3, in 12 innings, and was a 6-3 loser in the fifth game. But the old warhorse came back in relief in the eighth inning of the seventh game to pitch four shutout innings and earn a 4-3 win in the championship game. Johnson won two and lost one in a losing cause in the 1925 series against Pittsburgh. He won the opener, 4-1, and tossed a 4-0 shutout in game four. Two errors led to his demise, 9-7, in the seventh game. Johnson walked four and struck out 15, and had an earned run average of 2.08 in that series.

Johnson led the American League seven times in strikeouts, six in wins, and twelve times in shutouts. When the Baseball Hall of Fame opened its doors in 1936, he was one of the five charter members, along with Ty Cobb, Babe Ruth, Christy Mathewson, and Honus Wagner.

(Courtesy of National Baseball Library, Cooperstown, N.Y.)

Walter managed in the major leagues for five years after retiring as a player, and then became a gentleman farmer in Maryland. Aside from an unsuccessful run for Congress and one year doing play-by-play for the Washington Senators, Walter enjoyed the peace of Maryland's rolling hills in relative prosperity. He died from a brain tumor in 1946 at the age of 59.

Robert Tyre Jones

"Bobby"
May 17, 1902–December 18, 1971

The 1920s were a special time for sports in the United States. The era was blessed with heroes such as Jack Dempsey, Babe Ruth, Gertrude Ederle, Bill Tilden and Red Grange, who were the best-known people in the country. Bobby Jones shared the limelight with these headliners, and like them, became a legend in his sport.

It is difficult to imagine in these days of professionalism that the finest golfer in the first half of the 20th century was an amateur throughout his entire career. Bobby Jones' father was a lawyer, and provided Bobby with a fine education. Jones graduated from Georgia Tech and earned a law degree from Harvard. He was a natural on the links as a youngster, and at age 14 went to the third round of the United States Amateur Championship, after leading the field in the first round of qualifying play. Bob was so consistent at golf that from the time he was 14 until he was 28, no one beat him twice in championship play.

Robert Jones became a household name when, at the age of 20 in 1922, he won the United States Open golf championship. For the rest of the decade, Jones dominated the U.S. Open tourney. From 1922 until 1930, he won the championship four times, tied for first and lost the playoff twice, and finished second outright twice. Jones, always the gentleman, lost one of the championships because he called a penalty on himself, a violation that no one else observed. But Bobby was as tough a competitor on the final round of a competition as anyone who played the game. In 1926 he won the United States Open by gaining five strokes on the leader, Joe Turnesa, in the last nine holes to win by a stroke. Only in 1927 did he finish worse than second at the U.S. Open.

Unlike today's full-time professionals, Jones did not earn his living playing golf, but from his law practice. As a result he seldom crossed the Atlantic because the round trip took at least three weeks in those days, and that was too long to be away from business matters. However, Jones did win the British Open in 1926 and 1927, did not compete in 1928 and 1929, and won it again in 1930. In fact, he won it every time in which he competed. Bobby competed in 12 British and United States Open tournaments and was first or second in 11 of them.

Bobby Jones registered his famous grand slam in 1930, and then, at the age of 28, retired from competitive golf. "The Slam" in those days consisted of the British Amateur and Open and the United States Amateur and Open. Bobby won the British Amateur at St. Andrew's in Scotland, breezing through the final match 7 and 6. He won the British Open at Holyoke by

Bobby Jones in 1930, the year of his grand slam. (Courtesy of United States Golf Association.)

two stokes, and the U.S. Open at Interlochen, also by two strokes. The U.S. Amateur was captured at the Merion Cricket Club in Philadelphia when Jones easily won the last round of match play 8 and 7.

In later life, Bobby Jones became a successful businessman and continued to play in the Masters Tournament at Augusta, Georgia, an event that he founded. He was the first winner of the James E. Sullivan Award as the Best Amateur Athlete of 1930. Gene Sarazan, his contemporary, said of him, "Jones was great because he had the finest mind in competitive golf."

The game of golf has changed considerably since Bobby played it. The shafts are no longer wooden, the ball goes farther, and many excellent golfers make a living from the game. Yet once each spring, Bobby is remembered when the winner of the Masters dons the traditional green jacket and joins a tradition of excellence he established.

Jackie Joyner-Kersee
March 3, 1962–

Even when she was establishing herself as the finest female athlete in the world during the 1988 Olympics, Jackie Joyner-Kersee's accomplishments seemed to be overshadowed by her more flamboyant sister-in-law, Florence Griffith-Joyner. Many experts agree that Joyner-Kersee ranks second to Babe Didrikson Zaharias as the finest woman athlete of all time.

Jackie's success in the 1988 Games may have been downplayed because everyone knew that she was unbeatable. She was clearly the finest woman long jumper in the world, and when Jackie has seven events in which to compete, which she has in the heptathlon, eventually her ability will win out. Joyner-Kersee is so good an athlete that people take her for granted. They forget the hard work that is necessary to achieve her level of performance.

Jackie Joyner was born in East St. Louis, Illinois, a poor town across the Mississippi River from St. Louis. She was the second of four children in a family Jackie describes as "having a lot of love and caring." Her father was a railroad worker and her mother a practical nurse. Jackie was a good student and a great athlete in high school, and in 1979 she earned an athletic scholarship to UCLA.

Joyner's days at UCLA were happy and successful. She maintained a B average while majoring in history and communications, played basketball, competed in track and field, and met Bob Kersee, the head coach of UCLA's women's track team, and her husband-to-be. Jackie and Bob proved to be a winning team.

In 1982, Jackie won the NCAA heptathlon championship and earned the title of "finest female athlete in college competition." The heptathlon consists of seven events: 100-meter hurdles, high jump, shot put, 200-meter dash, long jump, javelin throw, and 800-meter run. Jackie qualified for the 1984 United States Olympic team in the heptathlon and won the silver medal at Los Angeles. Glynis Nunn, an Australian, nosed

The marvelous form of Jackie Joyner-Kersee. (Courtesy of Amateur Athletic Union.)

her out for the gold by a few steps in the 800-meter run, but Jackie was only beginning to mature as an athlete.

Joyner-Kersee set a new world record in the heptathlon in 1986, and won the prestigious Sullivan Award as the nation's most outstanding amateur athlete. In 1987, Joyner-Kersee began concentrating on an unusual double, the pentathlon and the long jump. She won both events at the 1987

Pan Am Games and repeated in 1988 at the World Games in Rome. She set world records in the long jump and 100-meter hurdles along the way. Her career peaked in September 1988 when she easily won the gold medal in the pentathlon and long jump at the Seoul Olympics. To appreciate how much better than her competitors Jackie is in the pentathlon, consider that she is the only person to top 7,000 points in this event, and she has done it five times.

Jackie won the Jesse Owens Award as the nation's outstanding track and field athlete in 1986 and repeated in 1987. She was runner-up to Griffith-Joyner in 1988.

Jackie is a well-muscled 5' 10", 153 pounds. She hopes to parley her good looks, brains, and reputation into a successful career in television when she finishes competing. Jackie has said, "I only dreamed of being the best I could be." Her best is good enough to be universally considered the finest female athlete in the world today.

Sandford Koufax

"Sandy"
December 30, 1935–

Sandy Koufax had two major-league careers; the former from 1955 through 1960 when he compiled a 36-40 record with the Dodgers, the latter from 1961 through 1966, when he put together some of the most scintillating seasons any major league pitcher has ever compiled. During his six peak seasons, Sandy won 111 games and lost 34 while compiling a 2.20 earned run average.

Sandy Koufax was a Brooklyn native who played the city game, basketball, while growing up. He was good enough at it to earn a scholarship to the University of Cincinnati. Sandy was brought up in a home where school work was important and, although he did not study much to the disappointment of his lawyer stepfather, he was a good student at Lafayette High School in Brooklyn. He starred in basketball, played first base and pitched some on the baseball team, and made up his mind that he wanted to be an architect. It wasn't until he started pitching regularly at Cincinnati and in the sandlot leagues in Brooklyn, that Sandy's talents caught the eyes of the major league scouts. He was signed by the Brooklyn Dodgers in 1955 for a $6,000 salary and a $14,000 bonus.

In many respects, the timing of his signing was a bad break for Koufax. The prevailing baseball rules required that any club signing a player for a bonus in excess of $4,000 was required to retain that player on the major league roster. The Brooklyn Dodgers won their only World

**Sandy Koufax pitching against the Minnesota Twins in the 1965 World Series.
(Courtesy of National Baseball Library, Cooperstown, N.Y.)**

Series during Sandy's rookie year, and with established pitchers such as
Don Newcombe, Carl Erskine, Johnny Podres, Clem Labine, and Billy
Loes, the totally inexperienced Koufax made only 12 appearances, pitching
41 innings and compiling a 2-2 record. With no opportunity to play minor-
league baseball, Koufax suffered through the unfortunate situation of
learning to pitch while sitting on the bench of a very good team. The learning process was slow, as Sandy's natural wildness was compounded by ten-
sion that caused him to grip the baseball too tightly. Sandy finally gained
confidence, and relaxed, in 1961. He also found home plate and combined

a blazing fastball with a wicked curve to become the terror of the National League.

Sandy was 18-13 in 1961 with a 3.52 ERA, and led the league with 269 strikeouts. The Dodgers finished second, four games behind the Cincinnati Reds. Koufax was leading the Dodgers to the 1962 pennant with a 14-7 record and a league-leading 2.54 ERA, when he was hit on the finger of his pitching hand in a game in June against Pittsburgh, and was sidelined for the season. The Dodgers lost the pennant to the Giants that year in a playoff.

Koufax was virtually unbeatable in 1963, compiling a 25-5 record, with an ERA of 1.88. His 306 strikeouts led the league. In the World Series, which the Dodgers swept from the Yankees, Koufax twice beat 24-game winner Whitey Ford, allowing the Yankees three runs in 18 innings. Sandy won the National League's Most Valuable Player Award that season as well as the first of his three Cy Young Awards.

The arthritis that abruptly ended Sandy's career after the 1966 season held Koufax to a 19-5 season in 1964, yet he followed that with spectacular 28-6 and 27-9 records to round out his career. Sandy struck out 699 batters during his final two seasons.

Sandy Koufax was only 31 when he decided that he risked permanent injury if he continued to pitch with the arthritic pain in his elbow. In 1972, he became the youngest player ever elected to baseball's Hall of Fame. For six years, he was as good as any pitcher who ever played the game.

Rodney Laver
"The Rocket"
August 9, 1938–

"There's no way you can play big time tennis," they told him, "you're too small, your legs are bowed, and you hold the racket in the wrong hand. You just don't have the tools." Rodney Laver proved them wrong. He turned himself into a tennis-playing machine who tracked down and returned everything hit into his court. He compensated for a routine serve with court speed and determination. He became so good, that he is the only person to win tennis' Grand Slam — the United States, French, British and Australian championships — twice.

At his peak, Rod stood 5 feet, 8 inches tall, and weighed a mere 150 pounds, but the left arm that wielded the racket was twice the size of his right. His style was simple: "Spin the ball ... Attack! ... Attack!"

As a young man, Rodney was lost in the crowd of great Australian tennis players until he defeated Neale Fraser in five sets to win the Australian national championship in 1960, his first important title. He lost in the finals at both Wimbledon and Forest Hills that year, but his performances in these events established him as an international star. In 1961, Laver lost in the finals of the Australian Championship to Roy Emerson, but defeated Chuck McKinley for the British title, and lost the United States Championship in the finals, again to Emerson.

Rod Laver was virtually unbeatable in 1962, and at the age of 24, established himself as the finest tennis player in the world. He swept the Australian, French, British and United States championships, a feat accomplished previously only by Don Budge of the United States in 1938. Ironically, he defeated an Australian in each of the finals, Marty Mulligan at Wimbledon and Roy Emerson in the other three finals. That year he also won the national titles of Italy, the Netherlands, Germany, Norway, and Switzerland.

Laver turned professional in 1963 and within two years established himself as the top professional on the circuit. The cream of the tennis-playing crop were all professionals in those days, and the touring pros included fifteen players who had been ranked number one in the world as an amateur. Laver won the United States Professional championship in 1964, 1966, 1967, 1968 and 1969, the French pro title in 1968, and the United States indoor pro championship in 1972. He also won the Professional Doubles championships in 1966, 1969, 1970 and 1972 with a different partner each time that included Butch Buchholz, Pancho Gonzalez and Roy Emerson. In 1968, in a major breakthrough, professionals were allowed to play with amateurs in open tournaments. Laver was again eligible to compete in the status events after six years of ineligibility. Laver won at Wimbledon that year as he warmed up for his second Grand Slam in 1969. He defeated Andres Gimeno in straight sets to win the final in Australia, and Ken Rosewall was a straight-set victim in France. John Newcombe and Tony Roache fell in four-set finals at Wimbledon and Forest Hills respectively.

So thorough was Laver's dominance of tennis in the 1960s, that he won the British title four times, 1961, '62, '68, and '69; the United States twice, 1962 and 1969, the French twice, 1962 and 1969 and the Australian three times, 1960, '62, and '69. Laver was a professional, and therefore ineligible to compete for these titles, from 1963 through 1967. Rod Laver won 63 national championships in his career that included 32 singles, 24 doubles, and seven mixed doubles titles.

Rod Laver is a successful businessman in Australia today and a regular in seniors competition. He still holds the racket in the wrong hand, so he is easy to identify. He also usually wins. Laver's advice to young tennis players is this: "If you're really serious about tennis and can invest about 22,000 hours on the court, you stand a fine chance of overtaking and beating me. By then, I'll be around 70."

Rod Laver after completing his first Grand Slam by defeating fellow Australian Roy Emerson at the U.S. Open in Forest Hills, N.Y., on September 10, 1962. (Courtesy of AP/Wide World Photos.)

Gregory Efthimios Louganis

1960–

Greg Louganis slowly climbed the ladder to the top of the 10-meter platform that September Monday night in Seoul, Korea, in 1988. He eased to the edge of the platform, thinking of nothing but the reverse three and one-half somersault dive he was about to execute. He needed a great dive, a good one would not do. China's sensational 14-year-old, Xiong Ni, had been almost perfect in all his dives, and had put the ultimate challenge to the greatest diver the world has known. A score of 85.57 would win the Olympic gold medal. Greg leaped high, twisted and contorted with the grace only he has shown from the platform, and entered the water with hardly a splash. The near-perfect score of 86.70 won the championship, and earned Greg the crowning achievement of his illustrious career.

Things did not come easily for Greg Louganis. He was born to 15-year-old high school students; his father Samoan, and his mother from the British Isles. Greg was given up for adoption at nine months. School days were an unhappy time for young Greg. He was a slow learner (later it was determined that he was dyslexic), and other children made fun of him because of his poor school work and because his skin was darker than theirs. He suffered from asthma, and to top it off, he was afraid of heights.

Greg was raised by his adoptive parents in El Cajon, California, a town near San Diego, where Greg's first interests were dancing and gymnastics. When Greg started to apply some of his gymnastic techniques on the diving board in the family's backyard pool, it became quickly apparent that the Louganises had a unique talent on their hands. By the time he was eleven in 1971, Greg had scored a perfect 10 at the AAU Junior Olympics at Colorado Springs, and had caught the eye of Dr. Sammy Lee, the 10-meter platform Olympic champion of 1948 and 1952. Four years later, Lee took on the job of coaching Louganis in preparing for the 1976 Olympics in Montreal. For the next 13 years, Greg totally dominated diving competition.

As a 16-year-old, Louganis finished second to Klaus Dibiasi of Italy, the reigning diving king, in the Olympic 10-meter platform event. Because of the United States' boycott of the 1980 Olympics, Louganis was unable to compete and lost the opportunity to pick up two virtually certain gold medals. Greg doubled in gold in the 3-meter springboard and 10-meter platform events in both the 1984 and 1988 Olympic Games, for a total of four gold and one silver medal in Olympic competition.

In addition to his Olympic conquests, Louganis has been a five-time world champion, and has won 47 national diving titles. From 1980 through 1987, he swept all three diving events, the one-meter and three-meter springboard, and the 10-meter platform, in six of the eight United States National Championships held. Greg is the only diver to score more than 700 points in platform competition, and the only one to score a perfect dive, seven tens, in both national and international competition.

As mentioned earlier, things do not come easily to Louganis. In 1979, in Tbilisi in the Soviet Union, Greg misjudged his takeoff from the platform and struck his head against it on the way down, knocking him unconscious

(Courtesy of International Swimming Hall of Fame.)

as he plummeted 33 feet to the water below. He quickly got over the physical and mental injuries the fall caused, and within a few weeks, was diving at peak form. During the first day of springboard competition in the 1988 Olympics, Louganis struck the back of his head against the board, opening a gash that required several stitches. He returned to competition without missing a turn, and won the gold medal in that event the following day.

Greg Louganis has a Bachelor of Arts degree in theater from the University of California at Irvine, and looks forward to an acting career. His muscular, 5 feet, 9 inch, 160-pound body has made him a popular pinup with many teenagers, and may be the ticket for a successful acting career that other great athletes, like Johnny Weissmuller, Sonja Henie, Jim Brown, and Alex Karras have found so rewarding.

Robert Bruce Mathias
November 17, 1930–

Bob Mathias entered 12 decathlons in his track and field career between 1948 and 1956 and won every one of them. In the process, he became the first of only two people to win the decathlon in two consecutive Olympiads.

Mathias was a 17-year-old high school senior in Tulare, California, when his track coach suggested to him that, with some work, he could qualify in the decathlon for the 1948 United States Olympic team in the upcoming tryouts. Bob had three weeks to get ready for the 10-event competition, and had never competed in five of them: the broad jump, javelin throw, pole vault, 400-meter and 1,500-meter run. Mathias put it all together to defeat his more experienced rivals and become the youngest track and field competitor to qualify for the United States Olympic team. By the time the '48 Games convened in London's Wembley Stadium, the world's best track athletes were no match for young Mathias. Although he won only one event, the discus throw, Mathias was so far ahead of the pack that he only had to jog around the track in the last event, the 1,500-meter run, to win the championship.

Mathias returned to the States as a national hero and was widely acclaimed. He won the Sullivan Award in 1948 as the Best Amateur Athlete. Bob enrolled in Stanford University where he excelled in the classroom and football, while continuing to win the National AAU decathlon championship annually in preparation for the 1952 Games.

Mathias not only won in Helsinki in 1952, but improved his performance in every event, raising his winning point score from 7139 to 8450. Bob Mathias was the first person to glamorize the decathlon and was also the first person since Jim Thorpe to earn the title "World's Greatest Athlete." Hollywood paid him its ultimate tribute when, in 1954, it produced *The Bob Mathias Story*. Bob was 23 at the time.

Bob continued to compete in decathlons as a member of the United States Marine Corps from 1954 into 1956. He then retired from active competition for a career in government work, first as a State Department goodwill ambassador, and later, as a four-term Congressman from California.

Bob Mathias in the long jump of the 1952 Olympic decathlon competition in Helsinki. (Courtesy of Robert Mathias.)

Mathias continued to make contributions to sports after his congressional career. In 1977, he took on the task of being the first director of the United States Olympic Training Center located at Colorado Springs, Colorado. Bob is proud of the fact that the first team that trained there was the victorious 1980 United States Olympic hockey team. Mathias went on from there to become the first executive director of the National Fitness Foundation.

The current era produces athletes who are trained to perfection, pumped up to artificial dimensions, and honed in specialized events. It is refreshing to recall how a 17-year-old youngster from California established himself as the finest athlete in the world and, four years later, proved it was no fluke.

Martina Navratilova
October 10, 1956–

Martina Navratilova was born in Prague, Czechoslovakia, in 1956 and grew up in Revnice, a Prague suburb. Both her mother and stepfather were tennis officials for the Czech government, and her grandmother was ranked number two in tennis in pre–World War II Czechoslovakia. Martina's stepfather coached her as a child and guided her through the very competitive world of Czech youth tennis. At 14, she won her first national title in age-group competition, and by the time she was 16, she was the highest ranking female player in her homeland. Martina, fully grown into her 5 feet, 7½ inch, 140-pound frame, was the number one ranking tennis player in Czechoslovakia from 1972 until 1975.

Martina was always fascinated with geography, and delighted in the opportunity to visit foreign lands, particularly the United States. On September 7, 1975, Martina announced her defection from Czechoslovakia to the United States.

When 18-year-old Martina defected, she had the potential for greatness, but lacked the temperament and desire to achieve it. She needed time to adjust to her newfound freedom, away from Czech tennis officials who had restricted her foreign play and frowned upon her increasing Americanization. Unfortunately for her, the teenager preferred fast foods to practice sessions, and soon ate herself out of playing shape. She also let defeats upset her to the point that she frequently became distraught, particularly when a streak of bad luck prevented her from winning the United States Open. Yet Navratilova was making an impact on the tennis world, and was rated among the top five in the world from 1975 through 1977. She won her first major tournament, the Virginia Slims Championship, in Oakland in 1978, and then won the British Open title at Wimbledon with back-to-back victories in 1978 and 1979. She teamed with Chris Evert and Billie Jean King respectively to win the Wimbledon doubles title in 1976 and 1979, and added the 1979 Avon and Colgate Series Championships to her growing list of wins. Martina was ranked number one in the world in 1979.

Martina took charge of her emotions, eliminated a few flaws from her game, and totally dominated women's tennis during most of the 1980s. She made the British Open at Wimbledon her personal showcase, winning it eight times between 1978 and 1987, including six in a row from 1982 through

Martina Navratilova's aggressive backhand made her one of the finest players in tennis history. (Courtesy of Carol L. Newsom/Virginia Slims.)

1987. Martina added the French Open in 1982 and 1984, and won the United States Open four times, and finished second four times, between 1981 and 1987.

Navratilova also won the Australian Open in 1981 and 1983, and the Canadian National Championship back-to-back in 1983 and 1984. The

Associated Press named her the Female Athlete of the Year in 1983. How dominant a tennis player was Martina in 1983? She played in 17 tournaments, won 16 of them, and had 86 wins and one loss, to Kathleen Horvath in the round of 16, in the French Open.

Martina became the greatest money winner in women's professional tennis, earning over $4,000,000. At her peak, she was so good in tournament play that, at one point, she won 55 consecutive matches. Martina made headlines when she lost.

Billie Jean King ruled the tennis world when Martina broke in, and was replaced by Chris Evert as the ruling tennis queen. Martina assumed that title during the 1980s until the emergence of Steffi Graf in 1988. Many tennis experts consider her to be the finest women's tennis player of the 20th century.

Paavo Nurmi

"The Flying Finn"
June 13, 1897–October 2, 1973

Paavo Nurmi, the quiet, almost sullen, running machine from Turku, Finland, was the finest track competitor in the world from 1920 until 1932. Nurmi was virtually unbeatable in every running event from the metric mile (1,500 meters) to 10,000 meters (6.2 miles).

Paavo became interested in running when his countryman, Hannes Kolehmainen, returned from the 1912 Olympics in Stockholm to a hero's welcome after winning the 5,000 and 10,000-meter runs, and the cross-country event. Paavo spent most of the next two years running alone, preparing for the day when his countrymen would recognize him. Nurmi claimed that he built up his endurance each day by chasing the morning mail train. He competed for the first time when he was 17, capturing the Finnish national junior cross-country championship. Paavo joined the Finnish army in 1918 and used the rigorous military training to further develop his endurance. In one contest, he ran 15,000 kilometers in 59 minutes, an impressive feat since he was carrying full army gear, including a rifle and 55-pound backpack.

Olympic competition was suspended in 1916 because of World War I, but when the 1920 Games convened at Antwerp, Belgium, the 23-year-old Nurmi was ready to take on the world.

Paavo finished second in his first Olympic event, the 5,000-meter run, losing to French war hero Jacques Guillemot, but came back to defeat Guillemot in the 10,000-meter run. He also finished first in the 10,000-meter cross-country run, an event no longer contested in the Olympics. Nurmi returned to Finland a national hero like his idol, Lolehmainen.

(Courtesy of AP/Wide World Photos.)

Between the 1920 and 1924 Olympics, Nurmi studied mathematics at the Helsinki Industrial School and perfected his running style. When he ran, Paavo was unaware of what his opponents were doing; he paced himself to run methodically against the clock. Breaking records was his goal, and en route to a record, he usually won the race. On June 21, 1921, Nurmi established the first world record, in the 10K event, and by the end of 1922 he had established new world records for 2,000, 3,000, and 5,000 meters. In 1923, he added the world records for 1,500 meters, the mile, and 3-mile runs.

Paavo Nurmi dominated the 1924 Paris Olympic Games. He opened by winning the 1,500-meter run in a time that was one second off the world record, and returned to the track 45 minutes later to win the 5,000-meter event, defeating his Finnish archrival, Ville Ritola. Paavo proceeded to win both the 3,000-meter and 10,000-meter cross-country races, and, most experts concur, would have won his fifth gold medal in the 10,000-meter run, but the Finnish track officials would not let him compete so that Ritola, the eventual winner, could share some of the glory.

In 1925 Paavo Nurmi made a grand tour of the United States and, for the first time, competed on the indoor circuit. He ran two or three events in each appearance, and won 53 of 55 races at all distances, smashing more than 30 indoor records along the way. His two defeats were to Ritola, at 5,000 meters, a race from which Nurmi dropped out because of indigestion, and to the great American half-miler Alan Helffrich in Yankee Stadium. Many experts feel that Nurmi burned himself out on the American tour, but as the 1928 Olympics will attest, he was still as good as anyone, although no longer totally dominant.

Paavo was in his thirties during the 1928 Amsterdam Olympics, but still was a world-class runner. He won the 10,000-meter run and finished second in both the 5,000-meter run and 3,000-meter steeplechase. He won seven gold and three silver Olympic medals in his career, and had set 20 world records, including every world standard from 1,500 to 10,000 meters.

Nurmi continued his career successfully until 1932, winning consistently in both the United States and Finland, and setting world records in the six-mile and 3,000-meter events. His plans to win the 1932 Olympic marathon, for which he was the favorite, were foiled when he was declared a professional for taking excess expense money.

Paavo lived a quiet life and shunned publicity. He was married briefly and had one son. He made his last public appearance in 1952 when he carried the Olympic torch into the stadium in Helsinki to the tumultuous applause of his countrymen. He lived in virtual seclusion after that for his last 21 years, until his death in 1973.

Robert Gordon Orr

"Bobby"
March 20, 1948–

Bobby Orr changed the game of hockey. When he was on ice, the Boston Bruins seemed to have four forwards and two defensemen, instead of the normal three and two. Although officially a defenseman, Orr was frequently called a "rover" because of his ability to participate in the offense while still carrying out his defensive assignments. No one in the history of the National Hockey League played defense at the same level as this 6-feet tall, 200-pound, lefty shooter. Orr's trademark was to rush the puck into the opponents' zone before they had the opportunity to organize their defense. His deft passes and powerful shot made him hockey's highest scoring defenseman. Bobby led the National Hockey League in assists five times in a career that essentially lasted nine years.

Knee injuries that nagged him constantly shortened Bobby Orr's career, yet his mark on hockey is indelible. He won the Calder Trophy as the National Hockey League's Rookie of the Year in 1967, and followed that up by winning the Norris Trophy, as the league's best defenseman, for eight consecutive seasons, from 1968 through 1975. Before Orr, defensemen were considered necessary, but their contributions seldom recognized. When Bobby started hitting the net as frequently as opposing forwards, hockey fans realized that Orr had brought an extra dimension to the game. Orr was the league's Most Valuable Player in 1970, 1971 and 1972, and won the MVP in the 1970 and 1972 playoffs, a first for a defenseman. Orr won the Ross Trophy as the league's top scorer twice, in 1970 and 1975, the only defenseman to ever win that honor.

When Bobby joined the league he had an immediate impact on the standings. Before Orr, the Boston Bruins failed to qualify for the Stanley Cup playoffs for seven consecutive years. In three years after Bobby arrived, they won the Cup, and repeated again two years later. Orr scored the winning goal in each of these championships.

Bobby Orr was born in Parry Sound, Ontario, a town of 6,500 people, about 150 miles north of Toronto. He started playing hockey at five in Parry Sound's minor squirt league, and consistently played in leagues with boys two years older than he. One coach, when he saw Bobby playing as a 12-year-old, said simply, "Orr was born to play defense."

The Bruins signed Bobby to a professional contract when he was 14 years old, and he spent his teen years commuting the 150 miles between his home in Parry Sound and where he played in Oshawa, Ontario. Bobby dominated the junior leagues for four years, playing against older and larger boys. Fans of the lowly Bruins heard for years of the playing skill of this teenage wonder, and anxiously awaited the coming of Orr. When Bobby was 18, and eligible for NHL play, he signed with the Boston Bruins. Bobby disappointed no one.

Orr's finest season was 1969–70 when he won the Norris (best defenseman), Hart (league MVP), Ross (scoring leader), and Conn Smythe (MVP playoffs) Awards, the only defenseman to win all four awards in the same season.

Orr's fearless play led to seven knee operations, and he was virtually finished as a hockey player after the 1974–75 season. Bobby appeared in only 36 games after that for the Bruins and the Chicago Black Hawks. He was elected to the Hockey Hall of Fame in 1979.

(Courtesy of Robert G. Orr.)

Arnold Palmer

"Arnie"
September 10, 1929–

Arnold Palmer's popularity stems from three ingredients: his face, attitude, and golfing ability.

Arnie was blessed with a face that expresses the full emotional range of every golfer—in fact, every athlete. When he misses a putt, millions feel the pain; when he strikes an iron perfectly, every spectator feels his elation as the ball trickles across the green to stop in birdie range. Palmer's face was created for television close-up.

When Palmer was at the top of his game, he and his fans felt that he was never out of a tournament as long as there was a mathematical chance to win. He would stroke one good shot and think, "If I can get going now, I can win this thing," a sentiment his fans shared with him.

The final ingredient, his game, is certainly one of the two or three best ever developed. Arnie earned 61 tour victories, including four Masters, two British Opens and one U.S. Open. He was runner-up in the U.S. Open four times, the PGA three, the Masters twice and the British Open once. Palmer was the first golfer to win one million dollars in tour money and was golf's leading money winner in 1958, '60, '62, and '63.

Arnold, the oldest of four children, was born in Youngstown, Pennsylvania, and grew up in Latrobe, a town about thirty miles east of Pittsburgh. His dad taught him golfing fundamentals well and Arnold frequently played golf with his mother, whom he described as "good for a woman and a real stickler for keeping a scorecard." When Arnold was nine, he carded a 45 for nine holes. In high school, Arnold developed into the best young golfer in western Pennsylvania, and he earned a golfing scholarship to Wake Forest University. In college Palmer was an outstanding golfer, and was the medalist twice in the National Intercollegiate tournament, although he never won the championship. After college, Palmer spent three years in the Coast Guard and then began a career as a salesman for a painting supply company. In 1954, he won the United States National Amateur Championship and decided to become a golfing professional.

Palmer's professional career started slowly. He won the Canadian Open and pocketed a purse of $2,400 in 1955. Because of Arnold Palmer, purses today are not so paltry.

Arnold won three tournaments in 1956, four in 1957, had off-years in 1958 and 1959, and set the golfing world on its ear in 1960.

The legend of Palmer's patented charge, and the formation of "Arnie's Army," began in 1960 when Arnold won the Masters tournament in Augusta, Georgia, and the U.S. Open at the Cherry Hills course in Denver. In the Masters, he birdied the 400-yard 17th and the 420-yard 18th to nip Ken Venturi by a stroke to win the coveted green jacket. In the Open, he rallied from seven strokes back, and passed 14 other golfers, to win in the last round. In that final round, Palmer was six strokes under par after the first seven holes.

Palmer does lots of things wrong on the golf course; his swing is too quick and flat, and he frequently finishes it up off balance. But he makes up for these flaws with determination and daring. He has both muscle and

(Courtesy of the Professional Golfers Association.)

grit. At 5′ 11″, 180 pounds, his wrists, forearms, and shoulders are as power-ful as any ironworker's. Yet Arnold's waist is so thin, that his constant need to hitch up his pants has become his trademark.

Golf has always been a major part of his life, yet he has found time to be a highly successful businessman with a corporate empire as extensive as any other athlete's. Arnold loves to fly his own airplane and play bridge. He is still active on the Seniors tour. He is easy to identify. He is the one with the army of fans behind him.

Oscar Palmer Robertson

"The Big O"
November 24, 1938–

Oscar Robertson invented the "triple double" in basketball. Before Oscar, no one consistently performed in double figures, that is, ten or more, in three categories: scoring, rebounding, and assists. Oscar averaged 26 points per game during his National Basketball Association career and had a season average of over 30 points in six of his 14 NBA campaigns. Scoring in double figures was routine to him. But the 6′ 5″ guard often collected more than ten rebounds in a game and dished out more than ten assists. Robertson was a complete player.

No one in basketball history could do as many things as well as Oscar Robertson. He was a team player, as his career total of 9,887 assists attests. That translates into just under 10 per game. He led the NBA in assists six times, and averaged an astounding 11.5 assists, during the 1964–65 season, while scoring over 30 points per game. He was a consistent 85 percent foul shooter, and led the league twice in foul shooting percentage.

Oscar was born in Charlotte, Tennessee, in 1938, but his family moved to Indianapolis when he was young. He learned basketball playing with his two older brothers at the local YMCA and a vacant lot near their home. Oscar mastered ball handling, and by the time he entered Crispus Attucks High School, he was accomplished in every aspect of the game. Attucks became a nationally known powerhouse with Oscar at the helm, winning the state championship twice, and at one point reeled off 45 consecutive wins. Oscar was all-state for three years and was selected as a high school all–American. He had major league baseball potential as a shortstop or pitcher and was a member of the National Honor Society, ranking 16th in his high school class of 171.

Oscar chose to play college basketball at Cincinnati University because it had a work-study program and he could help support his family while attending college. He alternated seven weeks of class with seven weeks of office work at the Cincinnati Gas and Electric Company. The Bearcats of Cincinnati knew that they had a prospect when Oscar averaged 33 points per game on the freshman team, an average he maintained during his three varsity seasons. Oscar became nationally known when, as a sophomore, he scored 56 points against Seton Hall University in New York's Madison Square Garden. Cincinnati won 80 and lost 9 during Robertson's varsity career.

Oscar co-captained the champion 1960 United States Olympic basketball team, one of the finest nonprofessional teams ever assembled.

Robertson played forward in college, but switched to guard when he

Oscar Robertson drives to the basket to score two for the Bucks. (Courtesy of the Milwaukee Bucks.)

joined the Cincinnati Royals of the National Basketball Association. In his rookie year, he scored 30.5 points per game and led the league with a record 9.7 assists, a mark that he topped six times. But playmaking was only a part of Oscar's game. He scored well, rebounded, and led. Every teammate's play seemed to improve with Oscar on the floor. Off court, Robertson served as president of the NBA's Players Association and was instrumental in revising the college draft rules and in establishing free agency for players.

Robertson played 10 years with the Cincinnati Royals, and although he made the perennial cellar dwellers a consistent playoff team, the NBA championship always eluded them. Robertson was traded to the Milwaukee Bucks in 1970 where he completed the final three years of his professional career. At Milwaukee he teamed with Kareem Abdul-Jabbar and their talents complemented each other perfectly. The 1970–71 Bucks became one of basketball's finest all-time teams, compiling a 66-16 regular-season record. They swept through the playoffs to the NBA championship losing only two games. Oscar was at his best at the annual NBA all-star games. He was selected to play in each season he was in the league, won the Most Valuable Player Award three times, and was runner-up three other times. He also won the league's Most Valuable Player Award in 1964, becoming the only non-center to win the award in over a decade.

When fans and sportswriters put their all-time NBA team together, there is debate at virtually every position. But any selector is safe when the name Oscar Robertson is penciled in at guard.

Jack Roosevelt Robinson

"Jackie"
January 31, 1919–October 24, 1972

Robinson bounced off third base, bluffing a dash for the plate. Whitey Ford, ahead by two runs, concentrated on the batter. Robinson suddenly exploded toward the plate, his 36-year-old legs churning like they did nearly 15 years before. The play was close, but Berra's tag was late, and Robinson became only one of 12 players at that time to steal home in a World Series game. The Brooklyn Dodgers lost that opening game, but the scene was set for their only World's Championship when they defeated the Yankees that year, 1955.

One measure of an athlete's greatness is the impact he or she made on the game. When Jackie Robinson became the first black player in the major leagues, the game was permanently changed. His aggressive play, desire, and leadership made him the bridge between old-timers, like Ty Cobb, and modern stars such as Pete Rose.

Jackie, the fifth of five children of Jerry and Mallie Robinson, was born in Cairo, Georgia, in 1919. His family moved to Pasadena, California, in 1920 when his parents' marriage broke up. His mother raised the family working as a domestic, and instilled a driving spirit in all her children. Jackie's older brother, Mack, was an outstanding athlete who finished second to Jesse Owens in the 1936 Olympic 200-meter run. Jackie followed Mack to Muir Tech in Pasadena, and Pasadena Junior College, where he starred in all sports. In fact, he even won the city's ping-pong championship in 1933. By the time he arrived at UCLA in 1939, Jackie was the best-known athlete in California.

Jackie, gifted in all sports, was UCLA's first four-letter athlete, starring in basketball, football, track and field, and baseball. In basketball, he led the Pacific Coast Conference in scoring twice; he averaged 12 yards per carry in football, and won the NCAA long jump title. The Olympic Games were not held in 1940 and 1944 because of World War II, but Robinson quite conceivably could have represented the United States in the decathlon had these games been held.

In 1941, Jackie starred in the annual all-star football game against the Chicago Bears and scored a touchdown against Papa Bear's professionals. He played professional football for one season, was an army officer during World War II, and then joined the Kansas City Monarchs of the Negro Baseball League, before getting the call from Branch Rickey to be the first black man in organized baseball.

People forget that Jackie was past his peak when he made his major league debut in 1947 at age 28. He could still play, however, and won the National League's Rookie-of-the-Year honors that year, hitting .297 and leading the league in stolen bases, as the Brooklyn Dodgers won the pennant. Jackie's best year was 1949 when he won the batting title, (hitting .342), stole 37 bases, hit 16 home runs, and drove in 124. It was an MVP year. Jackie had a career batting average of .311, and stole home plate 20 times.

Jackie Robinson was a winner. His Brooklyn Dodger teams won six pennants in his 10 years in the majors, after having won only two pennants before that in the entire 20th century. In 1962, Jack Roosevelt Robinson was elected to baseball's Hall of Fame.

Names like Josh Gibson, "Cool Papa" Bell, and Satchel Paige are not listed in this book because they never had the chance to play in the limelight. Jackie Robinson corrected that.

Jackie devoted his time after baseball to successful business, political, and race-relations endeavors. He died from diabetes complications at the early age of 53.

Jackie Robinson, basketball player, when he led the Pacific Coast Conference in scoring in 1938 and 1939. (Courtesy of UCLA.)

William Fenton Russell
February 12, 1934–

Bill Russell taught the National Basketball Association how to play defense. Red Auerbach, Russell's coach with the Boston Celtics, once said, "Nobody ever blocked a shot on the pros until Russell came along." But Bill

(Courtesy of Naismith Memorial Basketball Hall of Fame, Springfield, Mass.)

was more than a shot blocker; he was the final ingredient that made a very good Boston Celtics team into the greatest professional basketball team ever assembled.

Russell joined the 1956–57 Celtics that had the nucleus of greatness. Bill Sharman and Bob Cousy manned the backcourt, and a pure shooter,

Tom Heinsohn, was on his way to being named Rookie-of-the-Year. But Auerbach needed someone to play defense and get the rebounds that triggered the fast break, the trademark of the Celtics game. For 13 years with this early team, and when the Jones Boys, K.C. and Sam, took over the backcourt, and the great John Havlicek came on board, no one did his job better than Russell.

The Boston Celtics won 11 NBA championships during Russell's 13 years on the team. Bill Russell was an All-Star for 12 of those years, missing out in his rookie season when he spent a considerable part of it leading the United States Olympic team to a gold medal at the Games in Melbourne, Australia.

Bill was selected as the Most Valuable Player in the NBA in 1958, 1961, 1962, 1963, and 1965. He led the league in rebounds for four seasons. Yet, probably his greatest recognition came after his retirement. In 1970, on the occasion of the NBA's 25th anniversary, Russell was selected to the league's All-Time Team. In 1974, Bill was elected to the Basketball Hall of Fame. In 1980, he was again selected for the league's All-Time Team, this time for the 35th anniversary. In addition, the Professional Basketball Writers Association at that time voted him "The Greatest Player in the History of the NBA."

Bill Russell was not a great scorer; he averaged only 15.1 points per game during his NBA career. Bill essentially was a winner and a leader. He succeeded Red Auerbach as the Celtic's coach at the beginning of the 1967–68 season, and as player-coach won the league championship during his first two years.

Bill developed comparatively late as an athlete. Although he was 6' 7", he did not always start for McClymonds High School in Oakland, California. The University of San Francisco offered him a scholarship on the basis of his potential, and by his junior year, the clumsy, gangling kid had developed into the finest college basketball player in the country. The San Francisco Dons won 55 consecutive games on their way to back-to-back NCAA championships with Russell as the dominant force. Red Auerbach was impressed enough with Russell, now a wiry, 6' 10", 220-pounder, who high jumped 6 feet, 10 inches, and ran the quarter mile in 49 seconds, that he traded his high-scoring center, Easy Ed Macauley, and former Kentucky great Cliff Hagen for the right to draft him. It was the smartest move Red ever made.

Bill Russell is a sports legend who contributed as much to the Boston Celtics dynasty as any other person. He demonstrated that stopping the opponent from scoring, getting the rebounds, and being a team player are essentials for a great basketball team. If there is any doubt, try to find one NBA coach who would object to building a team around a Bill Russell at center.

William Lee Shoemaker

"The Shoe"
August 19, 1931–

Not all great athletes are six and one-half feet tall, and weigh more than 200 pounds. Willie Shoemaker is not quite five feet tall, and weighs 95 pounds, but has performed as courageously and skillfully as the best of the larger athletes. The "Little Giant" is the finest jockey of the 20th century.

Shoemaker's first sports love was boxing. As a youngster he competed as an 85-pounder in the 106-pound flyweight class, but despite his determination and boxing skill, he could not consistently give away 20 pounds to his opponents. He discovered horse racing by listening to the radio broadcasts of the major races in the Los Angeles area, and found his way to the tracks where he became an exercise boy. Soon he was getting his own mounts, and in 1952, his first full season, he won 388 races, tying him for first place among all the riders in the country. The following year he upped that total to 485, and became the nation's leading money-winning rider.

Shoemaker excelled at major stakes races, and winning the big ones enabled him to be the leading money winner in 1953, '54, '57, '58, and '64. His mounts have earned more than $120 million. By 1986 he had won 942 major stakes races, the all-time best in that category. Shoemaker won four Kentucky Derbies, five Belmont Stakes, and two Preaknesses.

Willie's skills with all types of horses and conditions enabled him to win more races than any other jockey in this century—over 8,800.

Willie Shoemaker was perhaps the smoothest-riding jockey ever, and his reputation for come-from-behind wins gave his backers the feeling that Willie's horse would always be close coming to the finishing wire. Willie prepared more thoroughly for a race than most of his rivals. No jockey studied his mounts' past performances and characteristics in more detail than Shoemaker, so by the time he mounted, he knew precisely what he wanted to do. Every railbird who invested a deuce on one of Willie's mounts knew that "the Shoe" would give it the full ride.

Willie had two special days in his riding career, Labor Day 1970 and May 3, 1986. On that September afternoon in 1970, Bill had only three mounts and won all three races, but what made it special was that these were his first rides after a 13-month layoff caused by a broken leg.

In May of 1986, the greying, 54-year-old veteran mounted Ferdinand, a 17-to-1 longshot in the Kentucky Derby, and gave the millions of onlookers a lesson in horsemanship. Breaking poorly from the inside post position, Ferdinand fell to last place in a field of 16 horses. Still dead last at the half mile post, Shoemaker guided the colt through the pack until he

(Courtesy of AP/Wide World Photos.)

was fifth with a quarter of a mile to go. Then with a bold move to the inside, Ferdinand poked his nose through a small hole at the rail, burst in front, and won by two lengths driving.

Bill Shoemaker, the oldest jockey by 12 years to win the Derby, shrugged off the well-deserved accolades with his usual modesty. When asked if it was his experience that won the race, he quietly replied, "No, the horse won it."

Shoemaker was still riding in 1989 after 40 years of mounting thoroughbreds. The 58-year-old admitted, "Look, I'm not as good as I was at 25, but I'm a lot better than a lot of 25-year-old riders." He was still good enough to win 60 races in 1988, his poorest year riding except for an injury-prone 1968, but he announced that 1989 would be his last campaign. Horse racing will miss a good one.

Warren Edward Spahn
April 23, 1921–

Who was the most effective major league pitcher in the second half of the 20th century? Feller, Palmer, Carleton, Koufax, Ford, Guidry, Seaver, Gibson? Not bad company, but as great as they were, none has a record to compare with Warren Spahn's.

No pitcher in the history of the major leagues was as consistent as Warren Spahn. Warren had 18 consecutive winning seasons because of his fine control and smooth motion. He won 20 or more games in 13 of them, tying him with Christy Mathewson for the modern-era, major league record. That is more 20-game seasons than Steve Carleton, Sandy Koufax, Whitey Ford, and Ron Guidry, the other great left-handers of this half century, have combined. Spahn won 363 games, more than any left-handed pitcher who ever played the game, and topped in this century only by Warren Johnson, Christy Mathewson, and Grover Cleveland Alexander. He accomplished this although he was 25 before he broke into the majors, having spent three potentially prime years in the armed forces. An average of only 15 victories a year during that span, a level far below Warren's standards, would have put him over the 400 mark, a plateau attained only by Walter Johnson and Cy Young.

"Spahnie" was born in Buffalo, New York, and learned baseball fundamentals from his father in their backyard. His coach at South Park High School converted him from a first baseman to a pitcher, and in 1940, Warren signed with the Boston Braves organization. By late 1942, he had earned a spot on the Braves' major league roster, but he was drafted into the United States Army during the winter of 1942.

Warren's military career was as distinguished as any major league player's. He was at the famous battle for the Remargen bridge over the Rhine River in 1944, and has been awarded both the Bronze Star and the Purple Heart. Spahn was the only major league player to win a battlefield commission during World War II.

Spahn returned from the war and was 8-5 with a 2.93 earned run average with the 1946 Braves, a good season, but only a hint of what was to follow. In 1947 he was 21-10, and in 1948 he teamed with Johnny Sain to lead the Braves to the pennant and world championship, and be heralded as part of the most famous pitching rotation of all time: "Spahn and Sain and two days' rain."

(Courtesy of National Baseball Library, Cooperstown, N.Y.)

Through 1951, he won 20 games each season, and even in an off-year, 1952, when he was 14-19, his ERA was under 3.00. At this point in his career, Spahn ceased to be an overpowering thrower; instead, he developed into an artist on the mound.

Warren played on three pennant-winning Braves teams, in Boston in 1948, and in Milwaukee in 1957 and 1958. His 4-3 World Series record includes a 2-hit shutout of the 1958 Yankees.

Spahn had exceptional control and a strikeout pitch. He led the National League in strikeouts for four consecutive years, from 1949 through

1952, and led the league three times in both earned run average and strikeouts. Spahn had only two seasons when he allowed more than 100 walks.

Warren Spahn was a remarkable physical specimen, lean and raw-boned, who performed effectively well into his forties. He pitched one of his two no-hitters when he was 40 years old, and in 1963, at the age of 42, was 23-7 with an earned run average of 2.60, including seven shutouts. He led the National League in complete games nine times, including seven consecutive seasons. Spahn was more consistent than spectacular which is probably why he won the Cy Young Award only once. That was in 1957, the second year the award was given. In those days there was only one award for both leagues, and no special award for relief pitchers. *The Sporting News* chose Warren as the best pitcher in the National League three times, in 1953, 1957, and 1958. Yet Spahn himself never fully realized how good he was. When he had won 300 games and still had 63 more wins remaining in his left arm, he said, "Walter Johnson . . . Christy Mathewson. Now me. It all seems so immoral."

The next time you select your all-time all-star baseball team, pencil in Warren Spahn as the starting left-handed pitcher. There was never a better one.

Mark Andrew Spitz
February 10, 1950–

Mark Spitz's seven gold medal performance in the 1972 Olympic Games at Munich is one of the great all-time sports accomplishments. Ironically, Spitz so thoroughly dominated swimming in his prime, that no one was surprised when he did it.

Mark Spitz was born in Modesto, California, in 1950, but his family moved to Honolulu when he was two, and he lived there until he was six. Young Mark learned to swim in Hawaii's blue waters, and was a well-advanced swimming competitor by the time he returned to the mainland. Spitz spent much of his preteen and teen years perfecting his techniques at the Sacramento YMCA, and the Arden Hills and Santa Clara swim clubs. By the time he was ten, Mark had set 17 national age-group records, and was considered unbeatable at that competition level.

Mark debuted internationally when he won four gold medals at the Maccabiah Games in Tel Aviv at age 15. At 17, he won five gold medals and set two world records at the Pan Am Games in Winnipeg, establishing himself as a favorite to be the swimming star of the 1968 Olympics.

Although maturing rapidly as a swimmer, Mark was still a youngster

Seven! Count 'em, seven. That's how many gold medals Mark Spitz won at the 1972 Olympics held in Mexico City. (Courtesy of Larry Crewell, *Bloomington Herald-Tribune*.)

emotionally, and his rebellious attitude annoyed coaches, officials, fellow competitors, and fans. He was a brooding, cocky loner and added a few friends when he publicly boasted that he would sweep every Olympic event he entered.

Mark won two gold medals in relays at the 1968 Games in Mexico City, and added a silver and bronze medal in individual events. Greatly disappointed, he returned to the pool and drove himself harder. He starred for Indiana University's swimming teams for the next several years, and quickly re-established himself as the finest swimmer in the world. Mark won the 1971 Sullivan Award as the outstanding amateur athlete in the United States.

When the Olympics reconvened in 1972, Mark was a 22-year-old adult who performed like no swimmer has before or since. He won seven gold medals in the seven events he entered, and a world record was set in each. The events were the 100-meter freestyle, 200-meter butterfly, 200-meter freestyle, 100-meter butterfly, 800-meter freestyle, 400-meter medley relay, and 400-meter freestyle relay. In 1968, Mark had predicted he would win each of his events. His prediction was accurate, his timing four years off.

Mark soon retired from swimming, and after a brief career as a television personality, became a successful real estate entrepreneur.

Each Olympics has its special star: Jim Thorpe, Jesse Owens, Emil Zatopek, Babe Didrikson, Bob Beamon, Wilma Rudolph, Mary Lou Retton, and Florence Joyner are examples. None shone more brightly than Mark Spitz did in 1972.

William Tilden

"Big Bill"
February 10, 1893–June 10, 1953

They called him "Big Bill" Tilden back in the 1920s although, by today's standards, his 6′ 1″, 155-pound frame would hardly qualify as big. He certainly was the finest tennis player in the first half of the 20th century, and many experts feel that he was the best player who ever lived.

Tilden's early life was tragic. Born into Philadelphia affluence, the proverbial silver spoon in his mouth, his family suffered one trauma after another, so that at the age of 22, he was the only survivor of a family of seven. After prep school, he entered Pennsylvania University where most of his classmates found him a brooding loner. He took up tennis seriously as a way of asserting himself, but it was many years before he fulfilled his potential.

Tilden was a late bloomer. When he was 23 he was ranked 70th nationally in men's tennis, and he was 27 before he won his first major championship. That was in 1920, but the tennis world was only beginning to appreciate the "old timer."

Bill Tilden toured Europe in 1920 and 1921, and demonstrated that the "gangling fellow" from across the sea was the finest tennis player in the world. He defeated Gerald Patterson, the great Australian champion, in the final round of the men's singles at Wimbledon, and went on to win all his Davis Cup matches on the continent. Tilden then returned to the United

(Courtesy of AP/Wide World Photos.)

States to win the U.S. Men's Singles from Aussie Norman Brookes, and thus became the first person since 1903 to hold both the United States and British titles in the same year. He completed the year by teaming with "Little Bill" Johnson to defeat Australians Brookes and Patterson in the Davis Cup finals.

Bill won six consecutive United States championships from 1920 through 1925 and added another in 1929. He won the British title at Wimbledon in 1920, '21, and '30, quite a record when one realizes that he did not compete there from 1921 until 1926. Bill never competed in the Australian national championship, and appeared in the French championship only once, in 1921, and won it.

Tilden may have lost a match or two between 1920 and 1926, but he won every prestigious event he entered during that period. He finally lost to the great French star, Rene Lacoste, in 1926, and by 1927, when he was 34, several of the top players could beat him. Yet Tilden staged a comeback in 1929 to win the United States Singles Championship, and won the British title in 1930, at the age of 37.

Davis Cup competition was the most prestigious tennis event during the 1920s and Tilden played on eleven Cup teams and was the driving force in seven United States wins. The U.S. was runner-up on the other four occasions. He personally won 17 and lost 5 in Davis Cup play.

Tilden played tennis like Arnold Palmer played golf in the 1950s and '60s. It seldom mattered where he stood after two or three sets. He loved to "mount a charge" and win in the waning moments. He was a master of all the strokes and possessed a fine serve, but excelled at baseline play. He is generally considered the shrewdest tactician the game has known.

Tilden was also an excellent doubles player. He won the United States Doubles Championship five times, even when he was paired with a 15-year-old youngster, Vinnie Richards, with whom he won the title three times.

A late starter, Tilden played remarkable tennis in his "senior years." At age 50 he played an exhibition with Ted Schroeder, the reigning U.S. Open champion, and beat him 6–2, 6–2. When Bill died in 1953, at the age of 60, he was still capable of beating many of the top players in the game.

Tilden loved the theatre and playing bridge. He was a top card player but his occasional acting ventures convinced the critics that tennis was his game.

In 1950, the Associated Press selected Bill Tilden as the top tennis player of the half century. Again in 1969, a group of international tennis writers chose Tilden as the best all-time tennis player.

Tilden's image was tarnished in many people's eyes when it was revealed in his later days that he had been convicted of homosexual activities with an underaged youth. When he died, most of his "friends" thought better of attending his funeral. Many tennis officials still consider him a nonperson. They choose to forget the person who made tennis the popular sport it is in the United States.

John Peter Wagner

"Honus," "The Flying Dutchman"
February 24, 1874–December 6, 1955

Honus Wagner is the finest shortstop who ever played baseball. He could run, field, hit, throw, and win better than anyone who played that critical position, and his selection as the all-time shortstop is seldom challenged. Baseball historian and statistician Bill James notes, "The selection of the greatest one ever at shortstop is easier than at any other position."

John Peter Wagner was a product of the coal mines in the Pittsburgh area. One of twelve children, he was born in 1874 in Mansfield, Pennsylvania, a town now called Carnegie. His German parents called him

Johannes, which was eventually shortened to Honus. Honus was loading coal when he was twelve, and by the time he was fully grown, hard work had developed his powerful physique.

Wagner made it to the National League as a utility player with the Louisville Colonels in 1897, four years before the American League was formed. In 61 games he hit .344, and followed that with seasons hitting .305 and .345. The Louisville club folded after the 1899 season and Wagner, and most of his teammates, were acquired by the Pittsburgh Pirates. In 1900, his first with the Pirates, Honus won the first of eight batting titles with an impressive .381 average, the highest of his career. That year he led the league in doubles with 45, triples with 22, and had a league-leading slugging percentage of .572. Wagner hit the ball as hard as any player in that dead-ball era, and led the National League six times in slugging percentage, seven times in doubles, three times in triples, and five times in runs batted in.

Wagner played outfield, second base, first base, third base, and even pitched once in his first four years in the majors, but in 1901 he played 62 games at shortstop, and it was quickly apparent that the position was designed for him.

Honus was a powerful 5′ 11″, 200-pounder, with a barrel chest, bowed legs, huge hands, and arms that dangled from his sides. People who saw him claim that his glove hand could reach anything hit to the left side of the infield. His specialty was back-handing a ball hit into the third-base hole, straightening up, planting his feet, and then unleashing a throw that always seemed to nip the runner. Old-timers also say that he made the play on the slow roller to shortstop as well as anyone who has ever played the position.

John Peter could run, and led the National League five times in stolen bases, as he accumulated 722 lifetime steals. He seldom struck out. Although accurate records on strikeouts before 1910 are not available, Wagner struck out only 327 times in 3,780 at bats during the last eight years of his career. When Wagner retired in 1917, he held the National League record of 3,430 hits, a mark that lasted until 1962, when Stan Musial topped it.

Wagner had a varied career after baseball. At one time or other, he coached baseball and basketball at Carnegie Tech, was sergeant-at-arms for the Pennsylvania legislature, and owned a sporting goods store. Wagner was a coach for the Pittsburgh Pirates from 1933 until 1951. When he passed away in 1955, Honus still held the National League records for games played, at bats, hits, singles, doubles, and triples.

Wagner became a charter member of the Baseball Hall of Fame in 1936 along with Christy Mathewson, Walter Johnson, Babe Ruth, and Ty Cobb. Two astute baseball people, both Hall of Famers themselves, Ed Barrow

The powerful swing of Honus Wagner that enabled him to win eight National League batting titles. (Courtesy of the Pittsburgh Pirates.)

and John McGraw, agree that Honus Wagner was the finest ballplayer each of them ever saw.

Johnny Weissmuller
June 2, 1904–January 22, 1984

In a 1972 interview, Johnny Weissmuller was asked whether or not he was a better swimmer than Mark Spitz. Johnny, never shy when talking about his accomplishments, answered, "I never lost a race. Never. Not even in the YMCA. The closest I ever came to losing was in the last lap of the 400 in 1924, when I got a snootful of water."

Weissmuller may have finished second once or twice in the backstroke, an event in which he competed occasionally, but there is no record of anyone beating him in a freestyle event in the dozen or so years he dominated swimming competition.

Johnny Weissmuller was officially born in Windber, Pennsylvania (although some claim he was born in Rumania and came to the United

(Courtesy of International Swimming Hall of Fame.)

States as an infant), and grew up in Chicago. His father was a captain in the Austrian army in the old country, and a coal miner, brewery worker, and saloon keeper in the United States. His mother was a cook. He learned to swim at the local YMCA and in Lake Michigan, and at fifteen, was invited to join the Illinois Athletic Club. Bill Bachrach, the Illinois A.C. coach, realized the raw talent he had in Johnny, and trained him in seclusion until his stroke was perfected. John debuted at the National AAU meet in 1921 and won the 50-yard championship. Johnny used an unorthodox style, his head and chest out of the water, but he propelled himself with a powerful kick that has yet to be matched. Over the next three years he was undefeated at every freestyle distance in which he competed, as he prepared for the 1924 Olympics in Paris.

Weissmuller was at his best during the 1924 Games. He won the 100-meter freestyle by nipping Duke Kahanamaku, who had won the event in both 1912 and 1920. He also defeated the great Swede, Arne Borg, at 400 meters, setting world records in both events. John also swam a leg on the victorious 800-meter relay team and, to show his versatility, won a bronze medal playing for the United States water polo team. At the age of 20, this relative novice established himself as the premier swimmer in the world. Johnny defended his 100-meter crown successfully in the 1928 Olympics at Amsterdam, and also won a gold medal in the 800-meter relay.

From 1922, when he set his first world records until he turned professional in 1932, he was clearly the finest swimmer in the world. At one time or other, he held the world record for every one of the 11 freestyle events then contested, including a 51.0-seconds for 100 yards, a record that lasted for 17 years. Weissmuller won five gold medals in Olympic swimming, a mark finally broken by Mark Spitz in 1972. No wonder the Associated Press voted Weissmuller the outstanding swimmer of the first half of the 20th century.

During his career, Weissmuller set 67 world records and won 52 national championships. He competed actively until 1932 when at 36, swimming professionally, he swam a sensational 48.5 100-yard freestyle.

When Johnny was a young man, he won a yodeling contest at a local Chicago theatre. This was an omen of what was to come, because Weissmuller is as famous for his second career as an actor, as he is as a swimmer. The 1932 film *Tarzan the Ape Man* was the first of 12 Tarzan movies he made between 1932 and 1948 that featured his patented Tarzan yell. Weissmuller considered the part perfect. He once said, "There was swimming in it and I don't have to say much." Later he also starred as Jungle Jim in both motion pictures and television.

John devoted much of his later days preaching two themes: learn to swim and stay fit. He was motivated to teach people to swim because as a teenager he witnessed a serious boat accident. Already a strong swimmer, John pulled 20 people from the water. Eleven of them died.

Johnny lived for a while in the fast lane and went through money and marriages as quickly as he cut through the water. However his sixth, and last, marriage endured for 20 years until his death in Acapulco, Mexico, in 1984. But fans will always remember his famous Tarzan yell, and his domination of swimming, for a longer period than any swimmer in history. And Johnny remembered the kids who did not have the chances he did. Upon his death, he willed his memorabilia, including his Olympic medals, to help retarded children.

(Courtesy of AP/Wide World Photos.)

Emil Zatopek

"The Czech Locomotive"
September 19, 1922–

In 1945 Europe lay devastated as a result of World War II. It seemed that the war had killed off another generation of youthful athletes. But at the Olympic Games held in London in 1948, the world was privileged to see the emergence of one of the finest runners who ever lived.

Emil Zatopek was nosed out in the finals of the 5,000-meter run in the 1948 Games, although his driving finish made up more than 30 meters in the last lap. But in the 10,000-meter run, Zatopek almost lapped the field to win by 300 meters in a time that was 48 seconds faster than the existing Olympic record. These performances were a foretaste of the greatness that was to come.

Emil Zatopek was born at Koprivnice, Czechoslovakia, on September 19, 1922. A product of peasant stock, young Emil worked in a shoe factory and saved a portion of his wages for tuition to a trade school. After trade school, he earned a degree in foreign languages and chemistry in Czechoslovakia's equivalent of an American community college. At college he developed an interest in the workings of the human body. Zatopek applied his theories to track, and developed a revolutionary training method. Since he was a member of the Czech army, Emil practiced wearing combat boots and a back pack, and ran alternating sprints with jogging, to relieve the boredom of the running regimen. Emil reasoned, "There is a great advantage in training under unfavorable conditions, for the difference is then a tremendous relief in a race."

Emil set his first national record in 1944, running 3,000 meters in 8:34.8. In 1946, he demonstrated the attitude that would make him great when he bicycled from Prague, Czechoslovakia, to Berlin, Germany, a distance of over 200 miles, to participate in a 5,000-meter run sponsored by the Allied Occupation armies. The unknown won the race before 65,000 spectators. In 1947 he won his first prestigious international race, beating Viljo Heino at 5,000 meters at the Finnish National Games, but he was still virtually an unknown until his 1948 Olympic showing. At that point in his career, Emil stepped up his training and became the finest distance runner the postwar world had known.

From 1948 until 1955, Zatopek dominated distance running as well as anyone ever has. In 1949, he set his first world record, at 10,000 meters. Emil set 18 world records in his career in distances from 5,000 to 30,000 meters. At one point he ran 20,000 meters under 60 minutes when, at that time, only four people had run 10,000 meters in less than 30 minutes. At the end of his career, in 1954, he set the world record at 5,000 and 10,000 meters on successive days. From 1951 until 1955, Emil held all eight official world records from 6 miles to 30,000 meters, and for three months in 1954 he also held the world record for 5,000 meters.

Zatopek was not only a record setter, but was equally good in head-to-head competition. Between 1949 and 1951, he won 69 consecutive races at all distances. He also had a four-year period in which he won 48 consecutive races at 5,000 meters, and six years in which he was undefeated in 38 consecutive races at 10,000 meters. Emil was rated number one in the world at 10,000 for seven years, at 5,000 for five years, and in the marathon once, 1952.

Zatopek's performance in the 1952 Games may be the finest recorded in Olympic history. He won the 5,000 meters so easily that one observer said, "Zatopek made a mockery of the race." Several times during the early going, Emil dropped back to the pack to encourage runners who were lagging behind, only to pull away when he was ready, to win going away in Olympic record time. He won the 10,000-meter run easily, beating his 1948 record by 42 seconds. Then Zatopek announced that he would run in the marathon, an event in which he had never competed. He won easily, beating the best previous Olympic time by six minutes. For the only time in Olympic history, one person won all three distance events.

Zatopek had a poor running style. It looked like the top half of his body was going one way and the bottom another. His face grimaced in pain, his head wobbled from side-to-side, and he huffed and puffed as he ran. The only thing he did correctly was to get to the finish line ahead of his competitors.

Emil continued to run effectively until 1956, and even was the favorite to win the Olympic marathon that year, until a hernia operation about a month before the face sidelined him. He still showed up and finished, and seemed to have a grand time being one of the also-rans.

Emil was always a pleasant person, an expert linguist, and very popular with the press. However, he sometimes gets vexed when his wife, Dana, teases him about who was the best athlete in the family. Dana Zatopekova won 13 women's national javelin titles between 1946 and 1960 and was the first Czech woman to win an Olympic gold medal. But even Dana will agree that she married the finest distance runner of the second half of the 20th century, and perhaps, the best of all time.

The Greatest

George Herman Ruth

George Herman Ruth is the finest athlete of the 20th century. No one else dominated a major sport to the extent that Ruth has. He was so good that, unlike his contemporaries, his performances become even more awesome as the decades pass.

A poll conducted by the Associated Press in 1950 indicates how the sportswriters and broadcasters evaluated the top athletes of the first half of the 20th century. We who live in the 1990s have the opportunity to put their selections into better perspective by considering how their performances hold up against the accomplishments of the modern-day stars.

Men	*Women*
1. Jim Thorpe	1. Babe Didrikson Zaharias
2. Babe Ruth	2. Helen Wills Moody
3. Jack Dempsey	3. Stella Walsh
4. Ty Cobb	4. Fannie Blankers-Koen
5. Bobby Jones	
6. Joe Louis	
7. Red Grange	
8. Jesse Owens	
9. Lou Gehrig	
10. Bronko Nagurski	

Of the women, only Didrikson's performances are still unsurpassed. She was the finest woman track athlete, basketball player, and golfer in her day, and given today's training methods and equipment, there is little doubt that she would excel in these sports today. Moody was a marvelous tennis player, but as the Virginia Slims ad campaign reminds us, the game has "come a long way" since then, and she probably would be hard-pressed to excel in today's competition. Stella Walsh is little known today and Blankers-Koen was a one-time phenomenon when she dominated the women's events in the 1948 Olympics.

Only Ruth and Thorpe would generally be considered "the best" still from the list of athletes from the first half of the century, Ruth for baseball and Thorpe for versatility. Didrikson is still generally considered the finest all-round woman athlete of the century, with Jackie Joyner-Kersee currently mounting a strong challenge.

141

Enthusiasts of current-day athletes can argue that Muhammad Ali or Rocky Marciano could take on either Dempsey or Louis. It is not clear who was the best of the heavyweights. Could Bobby Jones play with today's professionals? Obviously, yes. Certainly Bronko Nagurski and Red Grange would be stars in the National Football League today, and Gehrig would be the best left-handed hitter in the American League. In most instances, however, it is simply not clear whether the "old-timers" or the "moderns" would be better. They were both great, and thank goodness we have had the chance to see or read about them. And then there was Ruth.

When he first broke in with the Boston Red Sox as a 19-year-old rookie pitcher, George Herman Ruth was a burly, six-feet, two-inches tall and growing into his prime weight of 215 pounds. He had a huge chest and powerful arms and pitched with graceful ease. Even in his later years when he frequently ballooned to 260 pounds and his huge gut made his naturally spindly legs look like they could hardly support his girth, Babe still played as well as anyone who has ever played the game.

Babe Ruth played America's favorite game like no one before him or since. In a sense he had two careers, the first as a promising young pitcher, probably the best left-handed American League pitcher of his day, the second career as baseball's greatest hitter. For two transition years, 1918 and 1919, he was effective as both a pitcher and outfielder.

Consider the lifetime statistics of three great major-league pitchers, each a Hall of Famer, who had relatively brief pitching careers.

	W	L	PCT	ERA	STARTS	%COMP	HITS/ 9 INN	WALKS/ 9 INN	Ks/ 9 INN	ShO
A	165	87	.655	2.76	314	43%	6.8	3.2	9.3	40
B	94	46	.671	2.28	147	73%	7.2	3.2	3.6	17
C	150	83	.644	3.03	230	67%	8.8	2.0	5.3	26

Pitcher A is clearly the best power pitcher, with 40 shutouts, 9.3 strikeouts per each nine innings and giving up less than seven hits for each nine innings pitched. Pitcher B had a shorter career, but owns the best winning percentage, lowest earned run average, and highest percentage of completed games. Pitcher C had the best control. A manager would be delighted to have any of these players anchor his pitching staff. Pitcher A is Sandy Koufax and pitcher C is Dizzy Dean. Babe Ruth is pitcher B.

Of course, the icing on the cake for Babe is his 3-0, 0.87 ERA, World Series record.

There is every reason to believe that if Ruth continued to pitch, he would have been selected a Hall of Famer as one. With 67 wins before his 22nd birthday, he was well on his way to a 300+ career.

Now compare Ruth's batting statistics to Ted Williams', who is clearly the best batter since Ruth.

(Courtesy of UPI/Bettmann.)

	BA	SA	HR	HR%	BB	SO	AB	DBL	TRI
Ruth	.342	.690	714	11.6	2056	1330	8399	506	131
Williams	.344	.634	521	6.8	2019	709	7706	525	71

The batting averages are virtually the same with Ted getting a slight edge. Babe was clearly the better long-ball hitter with more home runs and considerably more home runs per at bat, plus a higher slugging percentage and more triples. Ted had more doubles and considerably fewer strikeouts. Their walks are comparable. It is interesting that both players spent most of five years as non-batters, Ted in the service, and Babe as a pitcher. There is a spot for both in any lineup card. Babe is generally regarded as a fine outfielder, with a strong throwing arm and a daring, if erratic, base runner.

Although his record of 60 home runs in a season and 714 in a career have been surpassed, no batter other than Williams approaches Babe's career statistics. Consider these facts about Ruth.

• His career slugging average is .690. Ted Williams is next at .634. Only three other players, Lou Gehrig, Jimmy Foxx, and Hank Greenburg, have career slugging percentages over .580.

• Ruth had a slugging average of .847 in 1920 and followed that up with a .846 in 1921. The third best seasonal slugging average was also Ruth's with a .772 in 1927. Babe also has the 5th, 8th, 9th, and 11th best seasonal slugging percentages.

• Ruth led the American League in slugging percentage 13 times.

• Ruth still holds the major league record for bases on ball in a season, 170, in 1923, and in total bases in a season, 457, in 1921.

• Ruth hit 50 or more home runs four times; no one else has done it more than twice.

• Ruth holds the record for runs scored in a season in the 20th century, 177, in 1921.

• Ruth batted in more than 150 runs in a season five times and scored 150 or more runs six times.

People think that baseball became more lively in 1917 or 1918 when a cork center was inserted and the ball was stitched tighter. But for many years, the ball was lively only for Ruth. Examine the statistics for the four years that Babe hit 50 or more home runs and compare his performance with his contemporaries for those years.

	1920	*1921*	*1927*	*1928*
Ruth	54	59	60	54
Best other in AL	19 Sisler	24 Meusel	47 Gehrig	27 Gehrig
		24 Williams	18 Lazzari	
Best in NL	15 Williams	23 Kelly	30 Wilson	31 Wilson
				31 Bottomly
AL total less Ruth	315	418	379	429
NL total	261	460	483	610

And in 1919, when Babe upped the major league home run record to 29, George Cravath led the National League with 12. Babe's teammates at Boston hit only four home runs, and four of the other seven American

League teams hit fewer homers than Ruth. His .992 fielding average was the highest in the American League that year, and he led the league in runs batted in, runs scored, total bases, and slugging average although he had only 434 at bats. Babe was second in the league in walks with 101. He stole seven bases, and in 15 starts, was 9 and 5 with 12 complete games. Babe never struck out more than 100 times in a season.

Babe was a fine pitcher and the greatest batter to ever play baseball. No one has ever excelled at both of these key aspects of the game. He was also outstanding at all the other phases of baseball. No one has dominated a major sport as has Ruth.

So here's to George Herman Ruth, "Jidge" to his friends. Babe, you were the greatest.

Index